Implications for Effective Psychotherapy with African Americans

Implications for Effective Psychotherapy with African Americans

Jay Thomas Willis, MSW, M.Ed.

INFINITY
PUBLISHING

ISBN 0-7414-5860-8
Library of Congress Catalog Number: 89-92511

Printed in the United States of America

Published December 2010

INFINITY PUBLISHING
1094 New DeHaven Street, Suite 100
West Conshohocken, PA 19428-2713
Toll-free (877) BUY BOOK
Local Phone (610) 941-9999
Fax (610) 941-9959
Info@buybooksontheweb.com
www.buybooksontheweb.com

DEDICATION

This book is dedicated to my sons, Marcus Jay and Martin Elliott, with hope that they will receive the stimulation, training, and development that will enable them to carry on the tradition of a strong African American family.

CONTENTS

Part III: Internal Dynamics

Part IV: Practical Approaches to Working with African Americans

Part V: The Future

FOREWORD

This volume considers the pathology that exists in the African American family from a slightly different perspective than most volumes. The author brings into focus his personal experiences and skills of observation, while shedding light on the African American family. He postulates that though African Americans have been emancipated from slavery for approximately one-hundred-fifty years, vestiges of that experience remain embedded in the behavior of descendants of those slaves, many generations removed from the actual experience. Though, many of our problems had their origin during the post-slavery period. He writes the book because of feelings that this point of view should be heard, but not necessarily accepted blindly, though he feels that his ideas are conceptualized correctly. Most of the ideas are documented from other sources, while some others are subjective—nevertheless valid. Some African Americans are not ready to accept the ideas put forth here, and for them it will take time to "frame" their minds to receive the ideas.

The author hints of a "Second Emancipation," in which African Americans will no longer perpetuate negative unconscious behaviors from slavery onto successive generations; thus, freeing the mind of the African American.

Implications for Effective Psychotherapy with African Americans contain psychosocial insights into the dynamics that exist in African American families, communities, and the society in general. It goes further than mere description: not only does it analyze these issues, but it also proposes solutions. It provides a historical review of the family as it progresses from description to analysis, concluding with a look at the future of the family. This book goes further than most others on the same subject, and provides the missing link as to what specific psychodynamic issues cause problem for the family and the individual, as well as how these issues develop and are maintained in a relationship.

It is important to read this book because it explains why African Americans have difficulty engaging in psychotherapy, and what can be done to successfully engage them. The historical conditions that led to the development of pathology are explained, and effective methods of dealing with them are explored. After reading this book you will be better at managing your own relationships because of a greater understanding of why your relationships are the way they are.

David R. Burgest, Ph.D.

PREFACE TO THE FIRST EDITION

This book begins by putting forth the idea that the pre-colonial African family was a healthy, viable, and functional social organization before being taken to the new world. Since its arrival, conditions have caused it to deteriorate, from the beginnings of slavery to the present day. Today, we observe the conditions of the family and simply label it as pathological, without taking into consideration the historical antecedents or what can be done to help it function better, also forgetting what caused it to be that way.

The idea is also put forth that the African American individual must become aware of what has taken place historically, so that inroads into his consciousness can be made. We must begin our education with the situation of the family in pre-colonial Africa and end with the conditions of the present day African American family, while realizing that a complete understanding of the African American family will require study which covers earlier periods in our history as well. It is important for those who are having problems within their family life to be involved in psychotherapy, so that an understanding can be attained of how to gain control of family relationships.

African Americans tend to resist psychotherapy because of historical relationships with traditional agencies. Efforts must be made by attempting a new approach to encourage them to take advantage of the many avenues for counseling that are available. Once they are in counseling, specific techniques must be utilized to keep them in counseling.

Many of the dynamics of African American family relationships are explored, and some individual dynamics are explored as well, since families are composed of individuals. Consideration is then given to the future needs of the family and the necessity of maintaining ongoing counseling efforts to keep the family strong and healthy.

The objectives of this book are to consider history and the part that it has played in contributing to the present conditions of the family, to look at some of these present conditions, and to give consideration to what can be done to negate the effects of history through psychotherapy.

This book would benefit the clinicians as well as the laymen concerned about the African American family.

African Americans have difficulty engaging in psychotherapy successfully, and this book explains why this is true and what can be done to successfully engage them. The historical conditions that led to pathology in the family are explained; effective methods of dealing with this pathology are explored; and the future of the African American family is considered.

PREFACE TO THE SECOND EDITION

The first edition of this book was my first attempt at publication, after I began to consider writing. I'm sure I originally made many mistakes in the first publication. I wrote this book almost twenty years ago.

This book is being revised mainly because of the criticism the first edition received. This revision is based on the criticism of one individual. Some of the criticism was negative, some was positive, but at least this individual thought enough to criticize it, and put it on the Internet. It is felt that some of it was deserved and some wasn't. I revised what I thought should be revised and forgot about what did not seem reasonable. I think the second edition is better for the criticism, and a more readable book overall.

When I first wrote the book, even with my neophyte skills, I wrote the book without much revision and published it as it was. For some reason I was anxious to publish it. At the time I did not have much experience at writing, and didn't realize that writing is mostly revision.

I mainly wanted to correct what the critic points out as Strunk and White errors, and to let someone more skilled at editing to edit it. For the most part I feel I did a good job on the first edition, but no book is immune to criticism. I thought the individual who typed the first edition had my back in regard to those Strunk and White errors, but apparently did not. I have gone over the second edition from stem to stern trying to make it more readable.

I didn't change or update any of the citations. Though they are outdated they still stand as truth for the period from

1974 to 1991, the time the book was written. The author believes that this point was proven with the citations used in the first edition. The book is based on my experiences during this period, and most of my references come from this period. I feel the references are just as appropriate today as they were then. The author feels that not much has changed in recent years in respect to psychotherapy—especially in relations to working with African Americans. At least some things have changed since the period for which the book was originally written, but most things remain much the same. My intent was to correct what I had already written, and make it more presentable, rather than add citations. The situation has seemingly gotten worse, since the education and employment has continued to deteriorate. This leaves the Black individual and family back in the hole again!

My intent for revising the book was to be sure the basic structure of the book was in order. I did make a few structural mistakes in the first edition that I have made every effort to correct in the second edition.

In revising the book the author decided that there were other articles I had written that would be appropriate for the book. I took three chapters from my book, *Finding Your Own African-Centered Rhythm;* and one chapter from another of my books, *Freeing the African-American's Mind.* I used them not to fill space, but because I felt they were relevant, and would add another dimension to the text.

Most of my insights are based on my readings as well as my experiences in private practice a number of years ago.

I have removed the words families and individuals from the title, and simply settled for African Americans.

A CRITICISM OF THE FIRST EDITION

Wanted: An Editor for Genesis Press, March 15, 2001

by

Thomas J. Burns

I purchased this work at the request of my students who correctly perceived that marriage and family therapists must practice with exquisite cultural sensitivities. I was initially surprised, even shocked, by the limited bibliography on the subject of Black family psychotherapy available to the practitioner from the general book market. Perhaps unfairly, the burden of identifying and researching "Black issues" has fallen upon the shoulders of the author, Jay Willis, and the small coterie of African American practitioners and researchers.

My second shock was the atrocious editing of this book. Actually, I am being kind. There is no editing. As best I can tell, most of the chapters are texts of addresses given at conventions, with no effort to avoid the maddening repetitions of the author's favorite themes. Not only is the logical progression of the book nearly imperceptible, but there is wholesale deprecation of the English language. One almost admires the chutzpah of this hearty soul who dares present a national publication without having made the acquaintance of Strunk and White, or Kate Turabian, for that matter. Lest one accuses me of literary exaggeration, I would point out that on page nineteen the author uses three distinctly different styles of source citation. There are a number of readers, I think, who will not get past the writing style, or the ghastly physical appearance of the text which resembles an underground life of Chairman Mao composed on a vintage typewriter.

My third shock was the author's bizarre attempt to reconstruct the pre-Civil War African American family, an effort that is far too short for the subject and far too long for this book. Some historians like Daniel Boorstin or Paul Johnson can color with broad strokes; Willis's brush is so broad it requires three men to wield it. Running with shaky research Willis depict the native African family experience as a virtual Garden of Eden, disrupted by the intrusions of slavers. This theory simply does not ring true in view of the long and painful demographic shifts that we can document from the European and Asian continents. Closer to home, studies of Native Americans reveal remarkable diversity and complexity. Willis's sketch of African Family life does not do justice to the richness and diversity of his subject.

The pity of it all is that Willis does have interesting things to say about the contemporary American racial scene, but this book actually gets into the way of his powerful opinions. He broaches controversial counseling issues with an almost reckless abandon. For example, he asks in so many words if slavery has, in effect, emasculated today's African-American male. He observes that Black women are pulling away from their male counterparts in the new economy and he states badly that Black women are becoming more vocal with their complaints that there are no Black men worth marrying. He discusses interracial pairings, distrust of "agencies," violence, addiction to risk taking, and poor schools as issues of particular pertinence to African-American counseling experience.

Willis is on target when he describes psychotherapy as a Euro-centered experience. It has long been my observation, too, that in African-American communities a troubled family is much more likely to turn to the extended family or the elders of the church than to professional therapist usually in the employ of "the system." Willis spends a lot of words to make the simple case that the therapist in an African-American setting needs to be a good case manager. His theory of counseling, when finally distilled, is a branch of the cognitive restructuring school. This is a richer insight than it seems, because the effects of racism are proportional to the way the victim thinks of himself. Some African-American clients are filled with rage; others manifest remarkable self-esteem and inner freedom. Willis puts great stress upon the therapeutic opportunities of changing self perceptions.

Willis bemoans the absence of African-American therapist in the United States, a condition that has not significantly changed in the decade since the book's appearance. {If anyone doubts this assertion, simply hang around a state's mental health licensing exam hall.} Given the fact that most psychotherapists will continue to be white for the foreseeable future, thoughtful analysis of the Black counseling experience is critical, particularly for those of us in the public health sector who engage routinely in transcultural therapy. Willis strikes me as the kind of practitioner who reflects upon what he sees and holds no fear of putting his controversial thoughts on paper. He has experience; he has courage; what he needs is an editor.

RESPONSE TO CRITICISM OF THE FIRST EDITION

I have disregarded some of Thomas J. Burns's criticisms, considering that some of his thoughts seem personal. I mainly tried to correct some of the so-called Strunk and White errors. Much of the criticisms seem a matter of personal style, personal perspective, and opinion. I feel the criticisms were harsh, but everyone has a right to their opinion. The criticisms did motivate me to redo the book. I also redid it because there were few left from the first printing. I probably did need an editor, but I didn't actually find very many so called Strunk and White errors—nor did my editor for the second edition. I proofread the entire book any number of times. Every effort has been made to follow literary traditions and conventions. There were a few so-called Strunk and White errors, and there probably still is—to the extent any book might possess some, but it was revised to the best of mine and the editor's ability.

The author depended too much on his typist in the first edition, for being responsible to edit the book—not being aware of what her credentials were. The typist did the best she could. I admit there was not much of an attempt to systematically edit the book. It was my first attempt at authorship. I was so pleased with myself that I forgot to do a more thorough editing job.

I don't see what having presented some of the chapters at conferences have to do with the quality of the text. He failed to mention that several of the articles were published in professional publications. Many books are written to be inclusive of chapters presented at conventions and conferences. I tried to change anything that I had repeated; sometimes I may have repeated things in a different way, but made use of very few blatant repetitions. Sometimes I did repeat points I felt strongly about. But I wanted those who read the book to get these points deeply ingrained into their unconscious. These chapters were also written separately, and it stands to reason that there might be some repetition. Repetition can be good in some cases. I have however reviewed the book and did my best to remove any needless repetition.

There is not meant to be a logical progression of the book, which was intentional, just chapters related to a similar topic. And I still cannot see what the critic called, "The wholesale depreciation of language." I feel the critic is exaggerating quite a bit. I have read Strunk and White many times. I don't use the Turabian style manual; I use the APA style manual, which I followed quite closely. Apparently the critic is not familiar with the APA style manual. If one looks at my citations on page 19, he would find I have followed the APA style manual to the letter for source citations and references. I apologize for the underground appearance, but it was the best I could do at the time. I have written the book in what I believe is a more commercial type style.

I guess you are dammed if you do and dammed if you don't. He describes my attempt to discuss the pre-Civil War African American family as being both too short and too long for the book. He said it was a bizarre attempt, but only said it was too short and too long. I may have been premature in my description of the pre-slavery African family—its problems did not begin in slavery—since the African family had been severely disrupted for over 10,000 years prior to the Atlantic slave trade. I noted this fact in the second edition. I don't quite understand what Native Americans' remarkable diversity and complexity have to do with the subject. I tried to present a realistic picture of African family life. I find Mr. Burns's criticisms at times nebulous at best.

ACKNOWLEDGMENTS

I wish to express thanks to my wife and sons: Frances Ann, Marcus Jay, and Martin Elliott, for their willingness to grant me the necessary time away from them to write and revise the ideas in this book, and for their support that has provided a greater understanding of what it means to be a part of a strong African American family. Martin Elliott and Marcus Jay also kept me straight on the computer. My last two computers didn't come with an instruction's manual. Whenever I made a mistake or hit the wrong key, I had to constantly be at their mercy.

Thanks to all those professors who provided the insight to begin to conceptualize and create my own ideas; they shall remain nameless.

Thanks to all those friends, acquaintances, and adversaries who, without knowing it, may have germinated some of the ideas found within the book.

ABOUT THE AUTHOR

JAY THOMAS WILLIS is a graduate of the University of Houston, Houston, Texas where he earned a Master's degree in social work; he is also a graduate of the Master's degree counseling program at Texas Southern University, Houston, Texas. He attended undergraduate school at Stephen F. Austin State University, Nacogdoches, Texas where he earned a B.S. degree in sociology and social and rehabilitative services.

He worked as a Clinical Social Worker for seventeen years, providing direct clinical services as well as supervision. He has been a consultant to a nursing home and a boys group home; taught college courses in sociology, family, and social work in community college and university settings; and has worked as a family therapist for several agencies in the Chicago area. In addition, he was a consultant to a number of home-health care agencies in the south suburbs and Chicago. Mr. Willis is a past CHAMPUS peer reviewer for the American Psychological Association and the American Psychiatric Association. He also spent a number of years in private practice as a Licensed Clinical Social Worker in the State of Illinois.

Mr. Willis has traveled and lectured extensively on the condition of the African American community. He has written twenty books, and written many Journal articles on the subject of the African American community. He has written several magazine articles. He has also written Op-Ed Commentaries for the *Chicago Defender*, *Final Call*, *East Side Daily News* of Cleveland, and *Dallas Examiner*. He currently lives in Richton Park, Illinois with his wife and son.

ALSO BY JAY THOMAS WILLIS

Nonfiction

A Penny for Your Thoughts: Insights, Perceptions, and Reflections on the African American Condition

Freeing the African-American's Mind

God or Barbarian: The Myth of a Messiah Who Will Return to Liberate Us

Finding Your Own African-Centered Rhythm

When the Village Idiot Get Started

Nowhere to Run or Hide

Why Blacks Behave as They Do: The Conditioning Process from Generation to Generation

God, or Balance in the Universe

Over the Celestial Wireless

Paranoid but not Stupid

Nothing but a Man

Fiction

You Can't Get There from Here

Where the Pig Trail Meets the Dirt Road

The Devil in Angelica

ALSO BY JAY THOMAS WILLIS

Fiction

As Soon as the Weather Breaks

The Cotton is High

Hard Luck

Educated Misunderstanding

Poetry

Reflections on My Life: You're Gonna Carry That Weight a Long Time

PART I

HISTORICAL CONDITIONS

Preliminary Comments

Throughout this book reference is made to the idea that pre-slavery, slavery, post-slavery, and modern times caused the incipient decline in the structure of the African American family. The devastation and havoc that was heaped on the family has lasted until modern times. It is understood that slavery had an impact, but all these historical situations continue to have an impact today, and many of the conditions haven't changed a great deal. The majority of African American families have never been able to reconstruct themselves and gain the necessary momentum to overcome the forces that were set in motion during these periods. Although, many Black families have been able to attain a standard of living that few whites are able to surpass.

It's difficult to say when racism, oppression, bigotry, prejudice, and discrimination began. They all probably began when we first made contact with other groups. By the same token our disunity, disloyalty, self-hate, and lack of group consciousness, as well as other problems, didn't just begin with slavery, but began much before that. The author argued with a fellow colleague once while teaching at a Southern university that our problems began in slavery, this was, before he expanded his reading habits. The author hadn't thought to look for causes prior to slavery. His colleague was right, because our problems began when other groups first set foot on the African continent. The author's orientation was limited at the time to what happened in slavery. Other groups began to explore other parts of the world approximately 10,000 years ago. It was then that other groups set foot on the African continent, according to John Henrik Clark, in *Notes for an African World Revolution: Africans at the Crossroads.* This is where our problems seemingly began. Everybody should know that Africans have been distraught since the first outsider set foot on the continent over 10,000 years ago. We know that various groups have since that time exploited African institutions and resources.

As Akbar has stated, "it would be rather simplistic and unidimensional to say or feel that slavery is to blame totally for the present condition of the African American family. We should realize that such causes are multidimensional. We can say for certain that the slavery experience has had a devastating and lasting effect upon the Black family."

If we are to make this claim, the burden of proof falls on African Americans to demonstrate what the pre-slavery African family was like, what the African family was like in slavery, and what the African family is like today. We need to see clearly what has happened to the African family that became the African American family. It is difficult to demonstrate a difference between what the African family is like today, and what the African American family is like today. They both have been exposed to similar kinds of colonialism which caused similar kinds of effects, resulting in disruptive processes for both families.

In **Chapter** 1 an attempt is made to demonstrate that the pre-colonial African family was quite different from the African American family of today. The pre-slavery African family was intact in most ways: It was basically healthy and productive, without the present forms of disorganization and the web of pathology currently observed in the African

American family. Though, as I have said, the African family has been deteriorating for approximately 10,000 years. It is necessary to present this picture because people want to know what the history of the African American family was like in pre-slavery times, when discussing therapy for the family and the conditions of the family today. Their consideration seems to be that if the family has always had major problems like the present ones, there is no reason to wonder why it is this way today.

However, because conditions were at least slightly better before the family had been transposed to the New World, there can be hope for a return to similar conditions. The African American family has the potential to be viable, healthy, and functional again. The disruptive processes the family has been exposed to have caused its major pathologies. Therefore, we need to come to grips with this fact and work toward modifying major problems that the family is experiencing today.

Chapter 2 continues with past, present, and future conditions of the African American family. An understanding of this history will help us to better conceive what must be done to begin to gain control over these pathologies. In any form of counseling or therapy, awareness is the first step toward solving the problem. We at least need to become aware of the historical factors involved.

This is why the chapters on "The Pre-Colonial African American family," and "Conditions of the African American Family: Past, Present, and future," have been strategically placed at the beginning of this book on *Implications for Effective Psychotherapy with African Americans*. These chapters should serve as a guide for a historical understanding of the African American family. With training and understanding, we can improve the situation in which the family finds itself. It is necessary to understand this history so that we can realize that help for some of us, over a long period of time, will be important in order for us to regain our equilibrium; this disequilibrium having been passed on to us by our ancestors.

We often discuss the African American family out of context, as if it had no history. This situation must be evaluated, if we are to understand and help the family to develop the necessary survival skills to continue to function as an entity. Out of our history grows our present behavior! For a complete understanding of the past, present, and future of the African American, a detailed study of world history is in order. *A little knowledge is a dangerous thing.*

Chapter 1

The Pre-Colonial African American Family

Introduction

African families were not uncivilized or primitive. It is necessary to first establish that the pre-colonial African family did not have an uncivilized or primitive form of family structure or existence before being brought to what later became the United States. They were not as well developed as some other countries, but did that make them primitive or uncivilized. They had well established and functional institutions. Also, the pre-colonial African family had not reached the state of degeneration and pathology that is presently affecting the African American family. They had their own way of functioning, but their institutions were viable, and supported their existence as family units. It is necessary to establish this because the claim made here and supported by history is that, after centuries of exploitation and maltreatment, the African American family has experienced a process leading to the present state of deterioration, disorganization, and pathology.

African American families do not naturally inherit a sense of pathology. If we were to look at Black families all over the world, it would be easy to state that the family inherits pathology; that there is something indigenous, endemic or genetic in the family that causes it to have various forms of pathology. The fact remains that Blacks have been colonized and enslaved all over the world and, thus, demonstrate some forms of pathology, in most cases. Pathology in the Black family exists to various degrees in different parts of the world, depending upon the severity of the form of slavery or colonization and the subsequent practices after it ended. Most Blacks have had a similar experience wherever they existed in the world.

European influence. It is not necessary to compare the pre-colonial African family with the present-day African family, nor the present-day African family to the present-day African American family. The reason is that where Europeans have intervened, the form of the family has changed, no matter what location is considered in the world. European influence is almost universal where the Black family is concerned. There is hardly any Black society that has not been exposed to some form of colonization or slavery. Therefore, it becomes difficult to compare a society that has been exposed to slavery with one that has not, in order to determine the differences in the way the family structure has evolved.

Modifying past degenerative processes. It is only important to compare the pre-colonial African Family with the present-day African American family. We can then begin to determine some of the degenerative processes that have taken place in African American family life. Consequently, we will discover what must be done to modify these processes that have already taken place.

A basic knowledge about the pre-colonial African family is necessary to realize what has happened to the African American family and, thus, develop strategies for intervention. We must be aware of where we came from before we can proceed with the future and be able to meaningfully restructure our family life. Once we have established that the African family during its pre-colonial period, was a strong, well-functioning, highly organized society; we can focus on what the African American family must do in order to return to a state of "normality."

Providing a general description. It would take volumes to discuss the family structure of each of the societies in West Africa, where most of the Africans were taken from to be brought to the New World. West Africa itself was too diverse to be limited to a brief explanation. However, a certain degree of consistency can be achieved through a general description of the structural family characteristics of the societies in West Africa. We must keep in mind that the attempt here is to provide only a brief general description and understanding of the characteristics of pre-colonial West African family life.

The Beginnings in Ethiopia

"Cradle of civilization." Egypt has been called the "cradle of civilization," and before 300 B.C., it distinguished itself as an industrial nation. It had, even during this time, a highly advanced civilization: well-developed political institutions, economic life, and social organization, as well as religion and art. The culture of Egypt and Ethiopia was extended in many other parts of Africa, as its inhabitants moved inside and outside of its borders. West Africa benefited by exposure to this magnificent civilization in Egypt and Ethiopia. Some of these features were present in West Africa when the Europeans and Arabs arrived (Franklin, 1969).

The coming of the Arabs. When the Arabs swept into North and West Africa in the seventeenth century, they discovered a civilization that was already advanced. West Africa had enjoyed limited contact for many centuries with other portions of the world. The culture they found was one that was indigenous to the area. There were many well-developed political states that had risen and fallen before contact with the East. Africa presented a civilization that ran the gamut from the most primitive to the most remarkably advanced; the people in West Africa being highly advanced (Franklin, 1969).

Other African invasions. Africans were invaded by several groups, who did so successively. Other groups had existed on the African continent prior to their separation many years before. We understand that all intelligent life, as we know it, began on the African continent. Other groups left and populated other parts of the world. It was 10,000 years ago when other groups began to explore that they rediscovered the African continent. Africans were subsequently under constant siege. The Africans were invaded by the Hebrews, the Greeks, Portuguese, the Arabians, the Persians, the Assyrians, the Romans, and others; as suggested by Chancellor Williams, in *The Destruction of Black Civilization* (1987). John Henrik Clarke also noted this fact in many of his numerous lectures and books (1990, 1991). Yosef ben-Johannan came to a similar conclusion in his book, *Africa: Mother of Western Civilization* (1971). Some invasions lasted for a long period and others for short periods. Africans were friendly toward these groups and invited them into their homes, families and society. We also allowed them to become part of our family structure. As John Henrik Clarke once said, "We are always inviting people to lunch, and end up becoming the lunch." We invited other groups to lunch in Africa many years ago when they first arrived on the continent, and we've become the proverbial entrée—there and everywhere else in the world since that time. We invited other groups into our society and gave them every amenity that we enjoyed. Subsequently, they infiltrated the African society and it has been on the decline ever since. Because of our gentle and trusting nature, other groups took control of the resources they could use and began a process of systematic destruction of what was not useful to them.

Impact of the invasions. Each invasion deteriorated the Africans' institutions and culture, and left us worse off than we were before. Once inside our society they proceeded to systematically dismantle the structure of the Africans' institutions, after they convinced the Africans that other groups' values and culture were superior and Africans' culture inferior. Africans assumed these individuals had good intentions. In many cases other groups were put in control. Once this occurred the individuals in power began to change the makeup of the various institutions. By the time the other groups had finished they had dismantled the social, political, economic, educational and familial institutions of Africans. Years of interference from outside cultures destroyed the very basis for African society, and we tried to replace it with other groups' institutions and values. Neither the Black family nor African society has been the same since. Africans were subsequently conditioned to self-hate, feeling their culture and characteristics were indeed inferior. These changes created havoc, chaos, and confusion that was internalized and passed on from generation to generation. Since that time other groups have maintained powerful influences which keep Blacks divided and in turmoil. The African society had been all but destroyed to the extent that we were vulnerable to the slave trade.

The African Family's Pre-Colonial Social Organization.

General characteristics. In pre-colonial Africa, the family was the basis of social organization. "At the basis of economic and political life in Africa was the family; the family had a powerful influence over its individual members" (Franklin, 1969, p. 28). Nothing was more impressive in the social institutions of Africa than the cohesive influence of the family. The immediate family undergirded every aspect of life (1969). The rule of discipline that was enforced by the male head of the family was responsible in large measure for the stability that could be observed in various aspects of life.

There were deep loyalties and attachments to the family that approached reverence by the heads of the families. There was respect for everyone in the family; it was sacrilegious to disrespect one's mother. The children cared for parents in their old age. Women were never considered unequal or second-class in their citizenship. The members of the family were very close, and there was a strong feeling of caring and concern, as well as promoting the welfare of the children (Fortes, 1950). The family was well organized and, without crowding, had privacy and felt very secure and protected. There were very few divorces, and if they did occur, the parents and community made sure the children were cared for. There was a profound bond between a child and both the mother and the father (1950).

<u>Descent.</u> There was a complex system of descent in which the eldest male was most often the head of the family. The descent was usually traced through the mother instead of the father. Children therefore belonged solely to the family of the mother, with her eldest brother as head of the family, exercising parental rights and assuming responsibility for the children's lives and actions. In other families, the head of the family was the biological father (Franklin, 1969). In many societies, descent was traced through the male lines. It was usually traced through either the male or female; only a few societies practiced double descent (Murdock, 1959).

Those forming the family consisted of all living descendants of the same ancestors; female of the matriarchal system and male of the patriarchal system (Franklin, 1969). The wife was not a member of her husband's family, and after marriage, she continued to be part of her own family who still had a majority interest in her welfare. The bride's husband was expected to pay an indemnity or provide material considerations to legitimize and stabilize the marriage. This was re-compensation for taking away a valued member and a guaranty that the husband would fulfill his obligation—it was not a purchase. The amount paid as an indemnity varied with tribal practice and position of the bridegroom (Franklin, 1969; Murdock, 1959).

It is believed that the African American matricentered form of family organization, which some behavioral scientists and others labeled as such, originated in Africa. The African woman had power equal to that of her husband, both in the family and in politics, and in some cases, had more. The idea here is that since descent was traced through the female line in many societies in West Africa, this value and concept was transmitted to the new world and, thus, became manifested in African American families. This phenomenon has been viewed as pathological; however, when examined from the perspective that this form of family organization originated in pre-colonial African culture and was considered healthy and viable, the idea does not seem quite as pathological. Contrary to popular opinion, a matricentered form of family organization did not cause the pathology that exists today in the African American family.

Diop (1978) puts forth the idea of a two-cradle theory with respect to matriarchy. His research leads to the idea that there are basically two distinct patterns of familial development: the matriarchy and the patriarchy. Both of these patterns developed out of distinctly different philosophies of family life. It was the different origins which led to the development of a matriarchy on the one hand and a patriarchy on the other. One form is not necessarily more primitive or better than the other, nor even later on the evolutionary scale than the other. Both a matriarchal and a patriarchal family form should be considered legitimate forms of family organization.

Forms of marriage. A household might be either an independent polygamous, monogamous, or extended family. Polygamy was permitted in most areas but was not universally practiced. In the extended family, there was one head, but a common residence (Murdock, 1959). Polygamy was the most common form of marriage, predominating in 88 percent of 154 societies (1959). The chief of the family paid the expense of the first marriage of a male member of the family. With the second wife the husband had to bare the expenses. Religion, in some ways, determined how many wives a man could have (Franklin, 1969). This was not limited by native religious practices, but the Moslems forbade adherents to take more than four wives. When Christians had influence, they insisted on only one wife.

Polygamy reduced the duties of each wife in the household, if the husband was without servants or slaves. The division of labor was so defined and the husband's duties so clear-cut that there was little friction resulting from polygamous relationships. Some advantages of polygamous marriages as they existed in pre-colonial Africa include: (1) No woman lacked a provider; (2) No wife had a problem in obtaining household help or a babysitter in time of need; (3) Every woman knew in advance what her position was, as well as future status, and had no fear of being superseded; and (4) The first wife normally had authority and prestige for a lifetime (Franklin, 1969).

This is not to say that polygamy would be a practical form of marriage for African-Americans. Forms of marriage are culturally relative. A discussion is merely provided here concerning what existed at the time; that this form was functional, producing healthy relationships and families.

Systems of residence. West African societies were usually unilocal in residence: one's spouse continued to live near or with his or her kinsmen and was joined by the other. Unilocal could be either matrilocal or patrilocal, meaning that the spouse would either live near his or her relatives. Each wife was established in a separate location and had her own material possessions; in this way, sources of friction were kept at a minimum (Murdock, 1959).

Rules of marriage. Custom dictated that each wife be treated equally, by eating and sleeping with the husband in regular rotation. Therefore, no humiliation was suffered because of favoritism (Murdock, 1959). The husband also had to be fair in sharing time and resources equally among all wives (Fortes, 1950).

Interaction with other groups. Other groups were ardent explorers, and generally left their women behind. They had a habit of taking women as concubines wherever they went. They therefore took African women as concubines, and sometimes married them. When offspring came from the marriage, the offspring generally took the side of their fathers, which gave the fathers leverage, but was not always in the best interest of African culture. This further contributed to the breakdown of African culture and society.

Transmittal of Pre-Colonial Family Values to the New World

Difficulty in transmitting values. There are those who believe that pre-colonial African culture had nothing to offer the New World. Yet, others believe that Africans brought a great deal of their culture with them, and that their cultural heritage can still be recognized in many aspects of American life. It should be understood that the Africans who were brought to the New World did not arrive devoid of language or culture, but it was hard to unite them with any kind of common bond. The slave traders made sure that those with similar cultures were kept apart and sent to different places, thereby preventing them from getting together. The plantation system made the survival of African family types impossible, except in diluted form. Nevertheless, some cultural family elements were transmitted to later generations of African Americans. It was difficult to maintain African family values and culture (Herskovits, 1958).

Some values that were transmitted. Despite this situation, the different cultures were similar enough that some aspects of the African culture were transmitted and maintained in the New World. Among the values that were transmitted are the following: (1) The concept of the extended family; (2) The idea of respecting one's elders as having wisdom and knowledge to offer which could guide and benefit younger adults and children; (3) The idea of considering the children as belonging to the community and the larger family and, therefore, everyone's responsibility; (4) Some elements of the family reunion in the African American culture have roots in Africa (Herskovits, 1958); (5) Elaborate burial and funeral procedures; (6) The idea that children are part of the community and, thus, cannot be illegitimate; (7) Common-law marriages; (8) Matriarchal form of family organization; (9) The idea of the importance of the mother being more highly valued than the father (This along with the idea of a matricentered family organization, may have come from the fact that in many societies descent was traced through the female.) (1958); and (10) Extensive network of cousins. These are just a few of the many values that were transmitted to the African American culture from Africa.

However, many of the values of the African family were prevented from flourishing in the New World, since the African American was limited in ability to participate fully in the new culture. The African had no choice other than to retain some aspects of pre-colonial culture. Though some pre-colonial values were passed on to the African American, it was difficult to maintain values in an environment that was inimical to the family. This situation severely limited the survival of pre-colonial African family forms and values in the New World.

The inability to hold onto old forms of family life, and not be in a position to utilize new forms, caused the African American family to experience chaotic conditions. This, along with their maltreatment and the conditions they endured, caused their family life to deteriorate. This deterioration has continued from the time the African was brought to the American shores to the present time.

<u>What was lost.</u> Upon having been cut off from the African culture and brought to a new culture without being allowed to fully participate in it, the African American was devastated with immeasurable loss. An attempt will be made to bring out in broad categories some of the things that were lost in going from one culture to the other.

Africans misunderstood other cultures and other cultures misunderstood Africans. Once societal structures were changed, there was a loss of traditional norms and values, with no sense of clear directions for the future. This resulted in confusion over what was acceptable, moral, and reasonable. Such situations are natural for breeding normlessness and conflict. When Africans became confused, chaotic, and disgruntled; we turned on each other, because our fellow tribesman made a readily available target. The ones directly responsible for the conflict weren't always available targets. Blacks took everything thrown at them and turned the hostility, anger, and frustration right back at one another.

This thrust into a foreign culture resulted in the African American losing his dignity, his self-respect, and to some degree, his Afro-centric perspective. The family not only lost its unity and cohesiveness, but its basic structure and function as well. It was no longer the center and foundation of the community. A sense of communalism was lost: the feeling that the community was a part of the individual, and the individual existed for the good of the community. A peaceful coexistence with nature, as well as a feeling that children belonged to the entire community rather than to the parents only, were lost. Many other African values and cultural traditions were also lost or transformed more into Western ways.

Strength of African American Families

Is the African family strong or weak? People such as Billingsley (1968), Hill (1972), Gutman (1976), and Staples (1970) have emphasized the strength of African American families, while others like Frazier (1939), and Moynihan (1965), have emphasized pathology and weakness. We are confronted with the idea of the family as being pathological and disorganized.

Hill (1972) discusses the strengths of the family. He says, what can be considered strength in one situation can be considered a weakness in another. However, several factors have been functional for the African American's survival, development and stability. Each of them is self-explanatory and can stand alone without detailed explanation: (1) Strong kinship bonds; (2) Strong work orientation; (3) Adaptability of family roles; (4) Strong achievement orientation; and (5) Strong religious orientation.

According to Hill, these things have kept the family strong and motivated to achieve, as well as improving its functioning. He does not believe that the family is any weaker or pathological than any other. The family, he says, has made a miraculous adaptation to the conditions under which they have existed and continue to exist, with more strength and stability than weakness and instability.

Summary

Without an understanding of the pre-colonial African family, it is difficult to comprehend what has happened to the African American family. We must be aware that the pre-colonial African family began to deteriorate when it first made contact with other cultures over 10,000 years ago. The history of the African American family must be understood before we can begin to make progress in our families, and the rest of society.

It is important, from this perspective, to focus on the mental health of each individual in our families. We need to develop our resources within the African American community in order to promote the welfare of our families. We must consider what we need to do to counteract the effects of generations of conditioning that were inflicted upon the African American, as a result of slavery and the conditions since slavery. An understanding of the pre-colonial family is necessary in order to give consideration to the development of appropriate interventions for the present and also the future.

References

ben-Jochannan, Y. (1971). Africa: Mother of Western civilization. Baltimore: Black Classic Press.

Billingsley, A. (1968). Black families in white America. New Jersey: Printice-Hall, Inc.

Clarke, J.H. (1990). Can African-Americans save themselves? Michigan: Alkebulann.

Clarke, J.H. (1991). Notes for and African world revolution. New Jersey: Africa World Press.

Diop, C.A. (1978). The cultural unity of Black Africa. Chicago: Third World Press.

Fortes, M. (1950). Kinship and marriage among the Ashanti. In A. Brown & D. Forde (Eds.), African systems of kinship and marriage. New York: Oxford University Press.

Franklin, J. (1969). From slavery to freedom. New York: Vintage Books.

Frazier, F.E. (1939). The Negro family in the United States. Chicago: University of Chicago Press.

Gutman, H.G. (1976).The Black family in slavery and freedom 1750-1925. New York: Vintage Books.

Herskovits, M. (1958). The myth of the Negro past. Boston: Beacon Press.

Hill, R.B. (1972). Strength of Black families. New York: Emerson Hall Publishers, Inc.

Staples, R.E. (1970). Educating the Black male at various class levels for marital roles. The Family Coordinator, 19, 164-165.

Moynihan, D.P. (1965). The Negro family: A case for national action. Washington, DC.: U.S. Department of Labor.

Murdock, G. (1959). Africa: Its peoples and their culture. New York: McGraw-Hill Book Company, Inc.

Williams, C. (1987). The destruction of Black civilization. Chicago. Third Word Press.

Chapter 2

Conditions of the African American Family: Past, Present, and Future

---

There is a growing need to explicate the conditions of the African American family from a historical perspective. There has been a proliferation of articles, as well as TV documentaries, discussing the dissolution of the family and the rift currently being experienced among its members. Newsmen and writers have discussed what is actually happening within the family at the present time with no references to what has caused the problems that are occurring within the family structure from a historical point of view.

After giving a brief introduction, the plan is to look at some of the historical antecedents, as well as present and future conditions, of the family. The purpose of this chapter is to shed some light on how slavery and conditions since slavery have affected the family in the past, and how they continue to affect it today. In short, why the family is the way it is, and what caused it to be that way.

A version of this chapter was presented at the Third World Symposium, Grambling State University, Grambling, Louisiana, and published in the proceedings of that symposium, March 1987. It was also presented at the Annual Black Family Conference in Louisville, Kentucky, in March 1987.

Background

The August 1986 special edition of *Ebony* magazine discusses poverty, unemployment, drugs, teenage pregnancy, discrimination, loss of religious values; lack of educational opportunities, inability to assimilate into the American middle-class white family value system that is incompatible with the realities of the African American community, and other contributory factors to the present situation of the family. Only an occasional reference is made to the historical antecedents of these problems. All of these are true problems experienced by the family, but they do not address the history of how African Americans came to be overwhelmed with these kinds of problems to such an exceptional degree. Other populations face some of these problems to some extent, but why the family has allowed these problems to permeate their being deserves to be looked at from a historical perspective.

Bill Moyers, on his CBS TV special, "The Vanishing Black Family" (1986), portrayed the condition of many families, but gave none of the historical situations that caused the family to be the way it is. This program was aired again in August 1989. The Black male was portrayed as an unconcerned, sexual being, concerned not with forming permanent ties, and only interested in making babies and moving on. The female was portrayed as satisfied with being his receptacle for sex and receiving welfare benefits. Whether or not this is true at this stage is irrelevant: It is important for anyone making such a portrayal to consider what conditions have led to this situation, if indeed the portrayal has any validity

In viewing the local PBS Channel (13) in Louisiana (1987), a live program called "Folks" documented women interviewees from the local area who stated that it was difficult for Black professional women to find men on their level. Many women were interviewed and seem to feel this way.

The following Sunday, men from the area voiced the opinion that African American women were in abundant supply and that an African American professional man virtually had his choice of women, whether they were professional or nonprofessional.

A nationally syndicated TV program, "Tony Brown's Journal" (1987), discussed the idea of whether or not it was difficult for a professional African American woman to find a desirable man. Many women who were interviewed felt it was indeed difficult to find desirable African American men, and felt this was true of African American women in general.

An article in the *Wall Street Journal* blatantly discussed the idea that a good Black man was hard to find (Sellers, 1986, p. 1). The following scene was described.

> PHILADELPHIA: Hundreds of people packed the ballroom of the Warwick Hotel here to attend a party for Black professionals. The ratio of women to men was five to one. Stunning hairstyles abounded, and elegant silks adorned slender figures.
>
> To the men, the selection was overwhelming. "I felt like a kid in a toy store," says Bruce Randolph, a marketing support representative for International Business Machines Corp., who attended the party. But, instead of mixing and dancing, the men mostly clustered together and compared notes. So, many of the women became wallflowers.
>
> Such scenes are symptomatic of a problem that many professional Black women confront everyday: A good man is hard to find.

This same article alludes to the fact that African American professional women have difficulty meeting an African American man who they feel they have much in common with. Though women have made significant gains in their educational and economic situations, they feel their lives are incomplete. One reason for that has to do with the fact that there are more African American women than men in any category, professional or nonprofessional. But it seems that there are significantly more professional women than professional men.

> Leroy D. Nunery, President of the National Black MBA Association estimates that 60% of the country's Black MBA's are women. A study by the College Board found that in recent years gains by Black women in such fields as accounting, engineering and law have far exceeded those by Black men (1986, p. 1).
>
> William J. Wilson and Kathryn M. Neckerman, sociologist at the University of Chicago, concluded in a study that Black women faced a shrinking pool of economically stable or marriageable men... Walter Farrel, education professor at the University of Wisconsin in Milwaukee, who has done extensive research on the topic, says the more prominent the successful Black woman becomes, the greater the chance she will end up alone (1986, p. l).
>
> The *Wall Street Journal* surveyed 50 Black women and 25 Black men who were professional and single, widowed or divorced. All the women respondents said they have difficulty meeting eligible Black men, and most said they have had to struggle to keep personal relationships intact (1986, p. 1).

Men seem to feel uncomfortable when they are in the position of not being dominant in occupation and salary. When women achieve in greater numbers than men in professional categories, it is another indication that the status of the men is declining. It is considered that because men function in a lesser status relating to occupation and salary, it leads to some unstable family situations.

Many single women are finding it easier to stay single and provide for themselves (Sellers, 1986). Harriet McAdoo, a Howard University social work Professor says, "That women's difficulty in finding mates and maintaining relationships threatens the future of the Black family" (1986, p. 1). "Today, fewer Black women marry, and those that do have fewer children" (Edelman, 1986, p. 54). Many of these women will remain childless, and the greatest number of children will be born to less educated and less affluent families (1986). "Some sociologists have speculated that the predicament of female-headed households feed on itself because boys (and girls) reared in such families may have no role model for marriage and fatherhood" (Poussaint, 1986, p. 50). It is well known that a large percentage of unwed mothers are in their teens, which creates an unstable family situation. Because of the economic family situation, it will be increasingly difficult for a poor family to buy a house or a car, or to put a child through college.

Frustration of African American Men and Women

All the evidence points to the fact that both men and women are very frustrated in their relationships. Many women have to consider alternative forms of relationships: interracial, single parenting, short-term inconsequential liaisons, and celibacy. Some have turned to various types of organizational affiliations. Some simply focus on their careers while discussing the problem with friends.

One young lady who was interviewed by the *Wall Street Journal* (1986) felt upset when she thought about trying to start a family; another considered placing an ad in a newspaper to help find a mate since she did not feel that men expected this kind of relationship to last. Still another young lady who was interviewed said that she would like to date an African American man but did not have the opportunity to meet any in her line of work (Sellers, 1986).

African American men who were interviewed by the *Wall Street Journal* (1986) felt no pressure to get into marriage and wanted to be more stable in their careers before marriage. Some tried to avoid getting serious by dating several women at a time. The following situation describes the feelings of African American men who were interviewed by the *Wall Street Journal:*

> A 33-year-old accountant in Atlanta says that, "Since there are so many single women around, I almost feel obligated to see as many as I can." Kevin Harvey, 31, a marketing manager of an industrial tool supplier in Rahway, N.J., says, "Right now, there are five women who I could get serious with and that's frightening" (Sellers, 1986, p. 16).

Many men date one woman for a short while and then move on to the next one. Some women are even afraid to identify their boyfriend in casual conversation, fearing that he may be seeing other women in the group. Experts seem to agree that men find it difficult to make romantic commitments and feel that this reflects uncertainty about career stability and long-term earning capacity. Many men and women seem to be into status: If a man is not an engineer or doctor, some women will not find him acceptable, or some men will tend to brag about how much money they make (1986). This kind of superficial behavior leads to various kinds of games being played.

African American Family is a Miracle

Again, very few authors actually discuss the historical antecedents of the family's situation and propose a theory as to what may be the causational factors for the present behaviors of its members. The family is truly a miracle: to experience the assaults of cruelty, brutality, and wickedness that the family has and yet retain any semblance of unity is a miracle (Williams, 1986). This survival experience has left some long-lasting consequences that have continued to affect the family.

Conditions of the African American Family Prior to Slavery

During the pre-colonial period, Africans had strong family ties. "A preliterate people, the West Africans nevertheless had a highly complex civilization. Their patterns of family life was close knit, well organized, highly articulated for the economic, social and psychological life of the people" (Billingsley, 1968, p. 48). Marriages were stable, and few were broken or made without family or community support. Africa had its problems, but the family concept was strong without deliberate assaults to disrupt the very structure of the family. The men and women who were brought to the New World as slaves came from "civilized" and "respectable" societies, though very different types of societies. The African family was much more closely integrated with wider levels of kinship in their society. The lives of Africans were severely disrupted in being involuntarily brought to the New World and being removed from their family and community structure (Williams, 1986).

The African society was very different from the European society that the African was brought to; but the African society had a long history of strong family and community life, every bit as viable as the European society. The

African was not being taken from a primitive, savage society (Billingsley, 1968).

In the West African society, from where most of the Africans were taken for the purpose of being enslaved in America, marriages united not only two people but two families, along with a network of extended kin who had influence on the new family; this kin network also had responsibility for its development and maintenance. The family was enmeshed in centuries of tradition, ritual, custom and law. "Family life was strong and viable, and the center of African civilization" (Billingsley, 1968, p. 40). The family was respected as the center of economic and political life.

There were well-developed patterns of descent, types of marriages, types of family, residential patterns, and patterns of child care protection. The African male had a strong and dominant place in family life assigned to and assumed by him. This place was dominant but not authoritarian, and was supported and guided, as well as limited, by custom and tradition; a substantial role was played by women (Billingsley, 1968). The children were well cared for because their care came from a wider kinship group rather than simply from the mother and father.

We were then snatched from our homeland, without a clue as to where we were being taken. After being captured by one means or another, sometimes sold out by members of one's own tribe, at other times captured in hard-fought battles; we became too weak to defend ourselves. Too often we were captured because we were too trustworthy. In any regard, it was a long, barefoot-thorny trek across miles of rough terrain to get to the ships that awaited us. We were driven in chains like cattle across this terrain to get to the ships. We suffered much abuse from our captors, and were forced to move on no matter the conditions or how we felt. During this trek, many Africans lost our lives from our homes to ships on the coast. Some were killed, some died of starvation. Many died because the trip was brutal, while others simply gave up and refused to move. Many died on this trek across the landscape; because of harsh treatment and outright murder. We were separated from the beginning to the end of the trip, and could do little about our condition, since we were overpowered. In most cases we were placed in chains, and had few means of escape. We were beaten and abused every step of this journey.

We were conditioned to a sense of self-hate and feelings of inferiority through degradation and dehumanization. Also we were conditioned to impotence and lack of unity, because of our inability to mount a successful collective response.

The transatlantic slave voyage between Africa and the Americas claimed the lives of approximately 1.8 million slaves over a period of about 250 years. This was a 1,500 miles ocean voyage across turbulent seas. The Middle Passage was a physical and psychological nightmare for an estimated 12 million slaves who were packed like animals aboard slave vessels. It was a terrifying experience. The conditions were miserable.

Slaves were usually shackled in pairs, the right arm and leg of one was chained to the left leg and arm of the other. They were separated according to culture, language, and tribe. We were confined below deck and packed into "slave quarters" throughout the ship's belly. We were stuffed in the holes of ships in quarters that were no more than six-feet long and not high enough to allow an individual to sit upright; much as sardines are packed in a can, in a way to fit as many as possible, and treated like animals—for many months of voyage. Slaves were forced to lie naked on wooden planks, and many developed bruises and open sores. The unbearable heat below deck, mixed with the human waste and vomit, produced an overpowering stench. Many of them died lying in their own excrement or the excrement of others. We sometimes slept next to others who had died because they could not stand the filth. The unsanitary conditions were breeding grounds for disease like dysentery, smallpox, flux, and measles; and there were all manner of other diseases. Close to 5 percent of the slaves died from diseases, and many more from malnutrition. Many were murdered for failure to comply with orders.

We existed in these conditions for many months at a time. If a ship feared capture by the authorities the whole cargo would sometimes be thrown overboard. We were fed twice a day rations of fish, beans, mush, or yams. Those who refused to eat, hoping to starve to death, were force-fed. Slaves were periodically allowed to come on deck for exercises in small groups, and to get fresh air. Women and children were frequently permitted to roam freely, and were often raped or abused by the ship's crew. There were occasional mutinies. Some slaves either starved or hanged themselves to death; some jumped overboard.

Many never saw any of their family members again. Those that lived passed on their experiences, and carried their psychological scars to their graves. Again, we were mistreated, abused, and misused every step of the journey. In this experience we were conditioned to self-hate, lack of unity, and impotence.

The African American Family in Slavery

Akbar (1984) asserts that there is both an advantage and a disadvantage in dwelling on the past, but those who deny lessons of the past are doomed to repeat it. We must realize that the past is a shaper of the present, and the hand of yesterday continues to write on the slate of today. Those who forget this leave themselves vulnerable by not realizing the impact of influences which do serve to shape their lives.

Slavery of the African American served as one of the saddest commentaries on man's inhumanity to man. The cruelty was unlike anything recorded in modern history. The atrocities of slavery have had a lingering effect, and psychological and social conditions from the past continue to call out from the genetic memories of those who survive until the present day (Akbar, 1984).

In elucidating upon the past conditions that have caused the family to exhibit its modern-day symptoms, several historical antecedents will be suggested as causational: (1) Mistreatment in slavery, (2) Welfare laws of 1950s, and (3) Residual discrimination and treatment after slavery. If we are willing to explore it, history demonstrates many ways in which the power structure has initiated situations which have placed handicaps in the path of families.

> To create an effective slave system, White America focused on destroying the positive self-image in Blacks destroying the Black family structure. In the process of trying to destroy the Black family White America forced inhumane conditions on the slaves... .The Black family has not completely recovered because many factors and behaviors from the slavery experience continue today (Williams, 1986, p. 3).

<u>The African American family was divided and restricted.</u> The family has faced severe difficulties since the first slave ship landed on the shores of the American continent. After each individual was captured in Africa and brought to America, each went separate ways. They had already been divided from the time they were first captured on the shores of Africa. The individuals were divided without respect to conjugal or consanguine ties. When the individuals

reached the American continent, they had already been successfully divided, but were disbanded again to separate points on the various plantations that were miles apart. Because of the distance the individuals would have to travel, as well as the lack of knowledge of the geographical area, the individuals would be unable to unite their families.

> … as soon as they landed in this country, slaves were immediately divided and shipped in small numbers, frequently no more than one or two at a time, to different plantations. This was the procedure with the very first Negroes brought to this country. It was found easier to deal with the slaves if they were separated from kinsmen (Frazier, 1939, p. 6).

Slaves also were restricted to life on the plantation and not allowed to travel from plantation to plantation unless they were escorted or in the presence of the slave owner. Each member of the family was taken to an auction and sold to the highest bidder, assuring that there would be few, if any intact families remaining since each slave was sent to different plantations.

"To make a Black African a slave, White America chose to destroy the Black family unit. Human rights such as marriages, family privileges, parental, and child relationships were not allowed to Blacks" (Williams, 1986, p. 9). In slavery, men and women were treated as property. Marriage was not registered with any official government agency or protected by law. Men and women were allowed to form a type of marriage, but this marriage was subject to being broken at any time.

In many cases, if a bond was being formed that the slave owner did not approve of, he would quickly forbid it or send one of the individuals to another plantation. If the forming of the family did not meet the purposes of the slave owner, families could be separated at any time and sent to other plantations (many of the family members never saw each other again), depending on what plantation owner made the highest bid. Most often, the mother, father, and siblings were sent off in different directions, making it impossible to maintain any rudiments of a family. Many mothers committed suicide because they did not want to be separated from their children. Some of them would even kill their children at the thought of never seeing them again. Since the slave owner did not sanction marriage between slaves, they had no remorse about separating the slaves (Williams, 1986). Nevertheless, the slave owner would often choose husbands for the woman and wives for the men.

It seems that "An effective way to eliminate the family concept is to destroy the dignity of its components; therefore, White America attacked the dignity of the fathers, the mothers, and the children of the Black family" (Williams, 1986, p. 12). The slave owner inflicted the most inhumane cruelty and instilled fear in the slaves so that they had no control over their lives. The slaves did not know feelings and relations; they only knew suffering and death. Though current attitudes and conditions (such as unemployment) feed these patterns and keep them growing, the origins of the African American family problems rest in the plague of slavery (Akbar, 1984).

African American woman during slavery. The woman did not have a choice over who would be the father of her child—this was determined by plantation economics (Akbar, 1984). "The slave-master would force the slaves to breed, so he could sell the children. Black women and men were valued by their ability to breed. In their attempt to further stamp out personal dignity, white men used Black women for their own personal sexual sickness" (Lerner, 1973, p. 46). "Blacks were used, abused, neglected and misused; as no other people in the history of mankind" (Williams, 1986, p. 17).

The woman had more flexibility in her role than the man during slavery, and because of this and the restrictions placed upon the man, she became the more stable element in the family. White America made the African American family a particular type of matriarchal unit. The male role was unstable and unpredictable. Any role that was allowed to the male was still controlled by the slave Master (Williams, 1986).

African American man during slavery. Historically, the man has existed in many situations that made it almost impossible for him to be viewed as a responsible, self-respecting individual who was in control of his family situation. The man has been promoted throughout history to the woman and the whole of society as someone who could not be depended upon in time of dire need.

> The powerlessness of the Negro man to protect his family for two and a half centuries under slavery has had crippling consequences for the relations of Negro men and women to this very day… a slave never has maintained an action against the violator of his bed (Billingsley, 1968, p. 61).

In most circumstances, the male counted on the female to negotiate for him because she had more of a relationship with the slave owner. In the minds of many, this was the beginning of seeds being planted which determined that the male was not dependable or trustworthy. The husband could not see his wife unless the slave owner permitted him to.

Furthermore, a young man had to obtain permission from the slave owner, in most cases, rather than from his or the girl's parents, before being able to court her. If the slave owner did not approve and the slave persisted in seeing the person, the slave owner would beat the person involved (Williams, 1986). Frequently, any type of stable relationship was discouraged because White America felt that this would interfere with slave trade or human breeding. Brown (1977) described the following situation:

> As soon as he felt able to go so far, that is about three months, he made another attempt to see her, was missed, pursued and caught. Then Thomas Stevens swore a fearful oath that he would cure him of "wife hunting." If he must have a wife, there was a plenty of likely yellow gals on the plantation for such as he to choose from. He might have his pick of 'em. But he (Stevens) wasn't going to let his nigger breed for another man's benefit, not he; so if John couldn't get a wife off the plantation he shouldn't have one at all. But he'd cure him of Nancy any how (p. 40).

"White America did not care about Black relationships and feelings when it came to making money" (Williams 1986, p. 12). This was very destructive to the man's personality and his feelings of being in control of his family, since he was not able to stand up for his family. It is this kind of situation which has had a long-lasting effect upon the ability of the man and woman to relate to each other and to nurture their offspring. This effect, it is believed, has lasted to modern times as indicated by the preceding issues discussed herein (Akbar, 1984).

The slave system was designed to destroy the manhood of males (Williams, 1986). The male was beaten in order to intimidate him. White America tortured and savagely mistreated the male until white America changed these survivors from warriors and family heads into subdued human beings. He had no choice over his mate, no legal marriage, no legal family, and no control over his children. "White

America took away the Black male's role as husband and father. Therefore, responsibility, discipline and direction for his family, including children, were not in his hands… not having the opportunity to determine destiny, eventually means that one will not. If not allowed to think, eventually one may not" (1986, p. 23).

Parental authority was in the hands of the slave master. The male was only a breeder and was so humiliated that he was not looked upon as a father or even a man. Slavery prevented the male from coming to emotional maturity by inflicting on him a perpetual childhood and imposing his master's will on him, resulting in his identification with the master: "The slave was the child and the slave-master was the father. In this 'boy' role, the Black male had to approach White America with bowed head… the slave-master and White America called the Black man a 'boy.' The slave was a perpetual child" (Elkins, 1963, p. 104).

A mother did not prepare her son for a stable relationship because she knew this would be disappointing. Some women continue to prepare their sons to be the type of men whose qualities they despise; such as having more than one girlfriend at a time. Thus, males in some circles feel good about seducing many women. If the male marries, the woman will have to contend with these qualities. Since the slave could not change his situation, he began to glorify it and, bragging about the many women he had impregnated, he glorified in being a "stud." He knew that if he became attached, he might soon have to leave and, therefore intentionally tried not to become attached. This lifestyle was passed on from the males of one generation to the next. Today, an African American man may have children by several different women and take no responsibility for any of them. He brags about this hit-and-run philosophy and feels that marriage is too restrictive. Williams (1986) says that:

> The Black male still prides himself as a breeder, loves to brag about being a father without having the responsibility of being a husband. The pressure is high, even today, on young Black males to establish themselves as potential breeders. As a young man, being a potential breeder gives him respect and acceptance with his friends and age group (p. 38).

<u>The African American child in slavery.</u> The slave child had no childhood and was trained to do what slaves do—be submissive and work hard. The slave child was robbed of any decent role models: Whom could he observe to develop roles for manhood? The slave child was simply trained to assume the role of a "boy" or, if female, to remain a perpetual "girl" (Williams, 1986).

<u>African American men and women during slavery.</u> The slave owner would threaten to sell, beat or even kill members of a family, if the man did not comply with the slave owner's wishes. The woman was used, in slavery, to keep her man in line. The slave owner knew that she would try to protect her man by helping to keep him under control and by making him think it was for his own good.

The woman then lost respect for her man because of his weakness and as a result of her own insistence that she maintain control, so that the family would be safe. When a woman has a man she cannot count on, she is likely to develop insecure feelings toward him, since a man is generally seen as a protector of women. Many African American women still have a pervasive insecurity toward African American men; these feelings come from a time when the man could not protect anyone not even himself.

The slave mother was also concerned about her son's survival, so she insisted that he be docile to white America. Again, "She prepared her son to be a good adult 'boy.' She encouraged his sexual masculinity… discouraging him if he suggested a change in White America's slave system!" (Williams, 1986, p. 35).

Was reason for mistreatment economic, social or political? It is felt by some that the slave owner was completely aware of what would be the long-term consequences of his actions in dividing families, though his motivation was probably more economic than social at the time. There is a saying among philosophers that *nothing is by accident and that everything is by design and inherent in the ways of man.* The behaviorist would say that, *all of man's behavior is purposeful and instrumental, either conscious or unconscious.* It would seem that it should have been easy to realize that irreparable damage was being done to the structure of the family and to their ability to establish and maintain lasting family relationships. It would also seem that the slave owner had to know that he was destroying the family while assuring less resistance to the building of his economic empires.

Nevertheless, in spite of his efforts, there was constant fear of slave revolts. By destroying the feeling of unity which is normally a part of the family structure, there would be less reason to be concerned about slave revolts. Regardless of the slave owner's intent, his behavior caused the same results for the family. It is certain that what has occurred during and since slavery has had a great impact on the way the family is structured today.

It is hard to understand whether the motive of the slave owner was purely economic, or if there was some social motivation for the purpose of directly affecting the long-term structure of the family. Coombs (1972, p. 41)) made the following statement in regard to the motivation for slavery: "Slavery has always been an evil institution, and being a slave has always been undesirable. However, the slave in America was systematically exploited for the accumulation of wealth." Slavery certainly seems to have had a denigrative effect on the structure and form of the present-day family.

African American males used as breeders. Another part of the situation that has had a lasting effect on the family structure was that the male was used simply as a "stud" to breed his mate, as opposed to being able to establish a relationship, "If the slave did refuse, he or she was beaten into submission. Often the slave owner would breed slaves who had never seen each other before" (Williams, 1986, p. 10). The male was mated with a female because the slave owner felt that by doing so he might produce a strong offspring who could do a good day's work (Akbar, 1984).

By using the male as a "stud" and dehumanizing him and the female in other ways, it justified to the slave owner that Blacks were part of a subhuman species and, therefore, it was ordained that they should be treated differently. It was to the economic advantage of the slave owner to treat the male as a "stallion." A common practice was to breed the slaves among the slave owners for various purposes. One slave owner during this period advertised the following:

> They are not Negroes selected out of a larger gang for the purpose of a sale but are prime. Their present owner, with great trouble and expense selected them out of many for several years past. They were purchased for stock and breeding Negroes, and to any planter who particularly wants them for that purpose, they are a very choice and desirable gang (Billingsley, 1968, p. 60).

Another account says:

> Slaves were treated like animals and bred like cattle. To the slave owners and White America, the female was just a cow, the Black male just a bull, and the

> Black child, just a calf. White America treated Blacks as though they were insensitive to pain, fear, and loneliness (Brown, 1977, p. 16).

Despite the way slave families were regulated, to keep them from doing so, they were still able to establish some strong family ties. Although the way the slave was treated led to a general lack of permanent relationships being formed between men and women, the man's subsequent behavior was to become quick to move on and leave the family, as well as to have difficulty forming long-lasting relationships.

The African American Family After Slavery

The family continued to experience much of the same treatment after slavery. It was even more difficult because the family was supposed to be free but had no means of economically stabilizing itself. The seeds had already been planted for a disorganized family life, but later in history, in the middle of the twentieth century, another act was perpetuated on the family that has had lasting results and further impact on present-day symptoms. Even though a great number of families had no other way of sustaining themselves, mothers on AFDC were not allowed to have a man in the home (whether husband or not, if "able-bodied"), and in many cases the father would leave home in order for the children to be able to survive. The Welfare System would enforce this rule by having what has been referred to as "Midnight Raids": The welfare worker would visit at late hours of the night to see if a man was sleeping in the home.

This type of activity has been well documented in the annals of history, as well as in a number of movies. Since the father or boyfriend was unable to find a job to help support the family, because of lack of training, lack of education or discrimination, he would sacrifice his own comfort so that the family could continue to receive welfare benefits. This situation has been used to further label the male as an irresponsible "character," when it was actually quite a self-sacrificing, altruistic, noble gesture. To the rest of society, this seems to be further evidence of how "lazy" and "shiftless" he was. It is also well documented that this alone caused many men to separate from their families and added to the idea that the African American family was basically a one-parent, "maternal" family. In a number of states today, a woman on AFDC cannot have an "able-bodied" man living in the household while she and the children are receiving benefits.

Intra-group differences. The question can be raised: If slavery is the cause of the pathological and crippling conditions of the African American family today, why then have some people been able to overcome these conditions while others have not? It stands to reason that if conditions were so poor, affecting family relationships so severely, no one would have been able to overcome the conditions. Some people use this argument to state that slavery, therefore, must not be the main cause of the pathological situation the family finds itself in today. However, this situation can be explained by the fact that there is always what Du Bois refers to as the "talented tenth." This means that there will always be a percentage of people who will survive negative conditions, no matter how bad, and do well in spite of them.

Aside from that, there were some African Americans who had preferential opportunities and were always free. Many were freed during slavery, and others bought their freedom and subsequently owned a great deal of wealth. For one reason or another, some always had better opportunities than others—though not equal to those of whites. It is still true today that some African Americans have better opportunities than others. In general, there will always be those who will rise to the occasion. However, this does not negate the effects of slavery on the masses of families.

Studies have been done to try to determine why some African Americans are able to thrive and have healthy family relationships while others are not. None of these studies will be discussed here, but the main conditions which have caused some individuals to become productive and to overcome are as follows: (1) Warm, nurturing, and supportive family; (2) Good basic education; (3) Cohesive community which provided mutual respect and support; (4) Exposure to a setting in which individual abilities could develop (Sowell, 1976); (5) Receiving appropriate discipline; and (6) Continuous support from a caring person, as well as a sponsor (someone to open doors that would not ordinarily be open).

All African Americans do not come from the same place, and both demographic and regional differences exist. This explains why they achieve at different levels. Sowell (1983) suggests, there are inter-ethnic differences because of these regional and geographical differences. One can assume by this fact that there might be intra-group differences as well. It then might depend upon the culture of the individual as to how well he is able to overcome. Indeed, Blacks from other countries have been exposed to different conditions from the African American, and thus might have a healthier perspective on life. When these people come to America, they maintain their cultural perspective, enabling them to do well within the American culture.

Present Conditions of the African American Family

The family is the most important unit in any society. Without a strong family, the marital pair cannot have good mental health and attitudes; the children cannot grow and develop in a healthy fashion. A stable family background gives a person a sense of place, a feeling of security, and a sense of stability. It is difficult to conceive of a well-adjusted individual who has grown up in a severely distorted and pathological environment. "Any system that deprives a people of its family structure denies the humanity of the people" (Williams, 1986, p. 7).

> It should be difficult to discern that people who, having been told for 200 years—in ways more effective than words—that they are subhuman, should begin to believe it themselves and internalize these values and pass them on to their children and their children's children. Nor, is it difficult to imagine how the history and current status of the Negro people might be different if, for all those 200 years our ancestors had been paid a decent wage for their labor, taught how to invest it and provided all the supports, privileges, and responsibilities which the new world offered its immigrants of Caucasian ancestry (Billingsley, 1968, p. 49).

Society has not made massive efforts to reconcile the damages of slavery and to bring the African American man and woman into the mainstream of the American society on the basis of equality. Not only has this not occurred, but many similar conditions continue to exist that existed during slavery (Billingsley, 1968). Slavery was a long time ago, and it seems that African American people should have overcome slavery, but

> The Negro people have never been indemnified, either economically, politically, socially, or psychologically for two centuries of bondage. And, furthermore, the wider society has not reconstructed itself to any substantial degree in any of these areas of life (p. 69).

Nobles and Goddard (1984) discussed the idea that slavery was not the single cause of the conditions of the family today. They felt that much of what we are has to do with the concept of Africanity. That is, some of our values and concepts have been passed on to us from Africa, and have to do with an Afro-centric perspective that we brought with us from Africa. So we are not simply an African people or an African American people alone; we are an African people within the context of an American culture. We have both an Afro-centric and a Euro-centric aspect to our values and concepts, which makes us more than simply being one or another. What ever we are is because of both perspectives. They criticized Frazier for attributing too much of what we are today to the conditions of slavery.

This brings some clarity to the situation, but still does not address the issue of a people being isolated on plantations and subjected to the will of the masters for generations upon generations. There were 300 years of this subjugation with very little outside influences. It should be considered that this might be enough to cause one to abandon former perspectives, and to let them take a back seat to whatever process of conditioning is current.

African Americans were encouraged to abandon whatever values or concepts they brought with them to the New World. They were immersed in a culture and forced to adapt its values—at least superficially. This was, in effect, a new beginning for the African American family. The values of the family took on new shapes and were molded to meet the needs of the slave master. It should be realized that some residuals of the Afro-centric perspective lie buried in the minds of all African Americans.

Willie (1981) feels that the African American family is still around and has not broken down. The miracle of the family is that it has survived and grown stronger over the years. There is evidence to show that there was very little opportunity for the family to fully experience family life during slavery; however, former slaves were able to form lasting relationships and family unions after slavery.

Willie (1981) denies that slavery is to blame for the conditions in which the African American family finds itself today. Contemporary situations and circumstances are to blame for this situation. He attributes income, poverty, continuous racial discrimination and other recent events as being linked to present-day family instability; feeling that few African Americans are affluent.

What also seems true is that all the factors Willie mentions as affecting family stability are somehow tied into conditions resulting from slavery. Few people would specifically agree that slavery is totally to blame for the present-day conditions of the African American family. Nevertheless, the conditions of slavery, combined with continuous patterns of discrimination, have caused the family to be the way it is.

Rising tension threatens stability. There seems to be agreement that a dangerous and rising tension exists between African American men and women; courtship has turned into a battleground. Men do not seem able to form commitments, and those who do want a commitment will sometimes run into a high-salaried woman who has been hurt once too often. These experiences make it difficult for a relationship to grow. This distrust and disharmony threatens to increase the already unstable family life. If parents cannot get along and communicate with each other, how can they produce strong, healthy children?

Elevation of professional African American women in occupations. A more modern twentieth-century example is provided of how the African American man continues to be affected by conspiratorial policies to dissolve his family:

Women are presented with more of an opportunity in many organizations to both enter and be promoted. They have been able to achieve a greater position for themselves in the work place than men, as a whole, especially in professional jobs, since women fill two-quota positions (double minority). In many cases, a woman will be considered for a job before a man. It is a difficult practice to evaluate its implications and long-term effects, but it does understandably put the woman in a better position than the man.

Since the woman has achieved greater status for herself, she has come to expect, in some cases, more than the man can provide, which causes problems for the entire family structure. Men become jealous of their women when it seems as though they are competing against each other in a survival struggle. Consequently, men and women have been confronted recently with tremendous difficulties in maintaining their family system.

In some cases, the woman has come to feel that the man is truly no longer dependable. This situation is considered by some as a modern-day attempt to further annihilate the concept and structure of the family. Furthermore, some authors believe that whites are less threatened by Black women than Black men. Consequently, the African American man is more systematically discriminated against, resulting in women being more occupationally elevated and a high percentage of men being unemployed.

Man expected to be "bread-winner." This culture, as well as most modern cultures, seems to designate the male as the head of the household and the family, meaning that he should be the "bread-winner." This alludes to the fact that he should at least command a higher salary than his wife. The male has been socialized in such a way as to experience a loss of self-esteem when he does not command this higher salary. There are two factors operating here: the female, being socialized to believe that the male should earn more money than she, begins to wonder if she really needs a man who cannot be the "bread-winner," while the male projects stronger feelings of this type onto the female, since his self-esteem is low and he is feeling insecure in the relationship.

This situation causes a lot of discord in the relationship. A man described one of his friends whose wife earned more money than he:

> The husband felt that his wife did not respect him very much while he earned a lesser salary. After the husband got a better paying job that significantly increased his salary, the wife could not do enough to give him as much respect as he felt he deserved.

Much of the change in the way the husband perceived his wife's response could have been due to the fat that he had more self-esteem and self-respect after his salary increased. Men who earned more than their wives will invariably say "who earns the most doesn't matter," but few men are able to accept this in reality. However, this kind of attitude on the part of the American male as a whole is beginning to change.

A man's concept of manhood is often tied into how much he brings home. When the wife earns more than he, it is not acceptable to him, in most cases. In this society, males are taught from childhood that if they are to be considered men, they must be able to pay the bills and meet the household financial obligations. When they cannot do this, many men are overwhelmed with feelings of uselessness and worthlessness. Eventually, the fight for self-esteem is lost, and they begin to view the wife and children as causing their inability to function adequately as a father.

<u>Economics as divisive force.</u> African Americans have had to survive under special conditions, but all families who

are poor have had to undergo difficulties related to economic survival. Poverty tends to be a strong dividing force in families, and a large percentage of African Americans are poor, which certainly causes problems for the family. Economic difficulties tend to be a strong force that affects the ability of a family to sustain itself.

In many cases, economics will determine whether a couple will get married, since it is expensive to raise a family, and even whether or not they will get a divorce. "Financial instability also contributes significantly to a Black divorce rate that is twice the White rate" (Poussaint, 1986, p. 50). The literature lists economics as one of the most frequent reasons for separation or divorce.

Poverty, in general, affects the ability of the African American man to maintain his family and has been an important factor since the beginning of slavery to the present day in this country. "Today's unemployment situation among Black males is the key factor contributing to Black male instability, if not the virtual impossibility of maintaining the Black male fathering role in the family structure" (Poussaint, 1986, p. 50).

After being conditioned. These behaviors, acquired during slavery, were passed down from one generation to another. Children of slaves picked up these behaviors from their parents and then passed them on to their children, and so it continues. These characteristics still exist in the family today, although modifications have been made by the social environment and situation.

Future Conditions of the African American Family

It seems that there has always been a dividing force operating to disunite the family. In spite of these situations that have been perpetrated upon the family, and regardless of whether or not they were intentional, it has been able to survive. This is because African American men and women have always been strong in the face of adversity and have the will to struggle, persevere, survive, and overcome.

African Americans today have an even stronger sense of family than past generations and are extremely dedicated to their families. We must be careful not to get caught up in the present-day myopia of society, feeling that we can do what is good only for ourselves. We seem to be experiencing narcissism, that is, we want what we can get "now," and we want to do "our own thing" without consideration or regard for others—families included. In order to keep the family strong, everyone must work to make it a reality.

African Americans not realizing the American dream. Many African American families have worked hard so that their children could participate in the fulfillment of the American dream and be able to benefit from opportunities that were denied to their parents. All Americans seem to share the dream that their children will get a better education, work a better job, and live in a better home. Some have been able to make this dream a reality. For a large percentage of children, the future does not hold the promise of success. "Black children are now more likely to be born into poverty, lack early parental care, have a single mother, an unemployed parent, be unemployed themselves as teenagers, and not go to college after high school graduation" (Edelman, 1986, p. 54).

Development of Hostility Among African American Men and Women

The female developed a hostile attitude toward her mate because of the role he played in slavery, which has not changed very much today. She seems bitter because she has had to play the dominant role in the family. The male internalizes the mother's hostility toward African American males. Women also get angry at the African American male because he has been taught well to behave as a "boy" in the tradition of slavery. The female needs to develop some understanding of how this development has occurred and has been maintained. Women should learn to support their men, while helping them to develop the necessary qualities.

The African American man finds himself struggling between his mother's influence, his mate's expectations and his own aspirations; partly because of the hostility he inculcated from his mother and the same feelings he picks up from his mate. Mothers educate their daughters to have a low expectation of marriage because of their own biases and hang-ups. The male and female must learn to be sensitive and receptive to each other, and they must also be patient with each other. Women sometimes get revenge on their husbands by influencing the children in a negative way against him—playing games that should not be played. This gives children the impetus to go into relationships with hang-ups.

The family should be viewed as sacred, and its members must develop trust for one another. The relationship between mother and father sets the tone for the family relationship. The old hit-and-run approach has created an atmosphere of distrust among women and is a response to insecurity on the part of the male. However, uneasiness and suspicion hinders growth in a relationship. The male and female need to learn trust that will eventually lead to honesty and commitment (Williams, 1986).

> Without trust, no relationship is safe. Trust assumes consistency and loyalty. White America also created as much inconsistency as possible to intimate slave

> relationships. It served White America's purpose well if slaves had a week system of trust (p. 53).

We must first call a truce and recognize that the problem lies not in each other; we must stop blaming each other. We cannot afford to keep setting each other up as "straw men." Social scientists generally agree that the problem is rooted in a traditionally racist society where African Americans are not accorded equal opportunities, especially in employment and education (Norment, 1986).

Summary

Both African American men and women have felt a sense of betrayal, which causes difficulty in achieving a high degree of stability in their family relationships. They are unable to trust each other: The woman feels that she will be used and "ripped-off," and the man feels that she has become part of the twisted conspiracy to undo him. These feelings come out of history and are due to relationships that men and women had during slavery; the woman being unable to count on her man during this period. These relationship patterns between men and women, which include lack of trust, have been passed on from one generation to the next. Coupled with that, many of the conditions of our society have not greatly changed in order to remedy the situation, so that men and women could change the basis of their relationships. In spite of all the negatives, the African American family is alive and well with many strengths. As African Americans, we need to understand the role that history has played in diminishing our family life, while making an attempt to regain its equilibrium.

References

Akbar, N. (1984). Chains and images of psychological slavery. New Jersey: New Mind Productions.

Billingsley, A. (1968). Black families in white America. New Jersey: Prentice-Hall, Inc.

Brown, J. (1977). Slave life in Georgia: A narrative of the life, suffering, and escape of John Brown, a fugitive slave, now in England. London: Ayer Company Publishers.

Coombs, N. (1972). The Black experience in America. New York: Twayne Publishers, Inc.

Edelman, M.W. (1986, August). Save the children. Ebony, pp. 53-58.

Elkins, S.M. (1963). Slavery: A problem in American institutional and intellectual life. New York: Grosset and Dunlap, Inc.

Frazier, F.E. (1939). The Negro family in the United States. Chicago: University of Chicago Press.

Lerner, G. (1973). Black women in white America: A documentary history. New York: Vintage Books.

Nobles, W.W., & Goddard, L.L. (1984). Understanding the Black family: A guide for scholarship and research. Oakland: A Black Family Institute Publication.

Norment, L. (1986, August). Resolve tension between Black men and women. Ebony, pp. 153-156.

Poussaint, A.F. (1986, August). Save the fathers. Ebony, pp. 43-50.

Sellers, V. (1986, May 16). Dating game. The Wall Street Journal, pp. 1, 16.

Sowell, T. (1983). The economic and politics of race. New York: William Morrow and Company, Inc.

Sowell, T. (1976). Patterns of Black excellence. Washington, D.C.: Ethnics and Public Policy Center.

Williams, R. (1986). They stole it but you must return it. New York: Hema Publishing Co.

Willie, C.V. (1981). A new look at Black families. New York: General Hall, Inc.

PART II

TREATING THE FAMILY

Preliminary Comments

The African American family seems to have a natural aversion to counseling; much of this comes from a time when the family was receiving services in mostly all white agencies, and they did not believe they were being treated with respect nor receiving good benefits. These individuals felt that counselors tended to pry into their business, and the information sought was more of a private matter, unrelated to the request for services.

In Chapter 3, consideration is given to the counselor's role within the African-American community. It is noted that the African American has always invested the role of the counselor in the church or in a small group of relatives and friends—even neighbors. Anyone outside this group was considered an outsider and not in their network of association. They do not consider it healthy to share personal feelings with strangers and have always utilized these kinds of self-help networks rather than relying on traditional agencies for help.

African Americans only utilize these traditional agencies when forced by the school, police, or other institutions within the community. Even when they come to these agencies, it is always with some reluctance. Women have always been less threatened by these agencies than men.

Men consider it as a challenge to their manhood to seek help and admit that they cannot deal with a problem.

Some therapists believe "counseling is counseling" and that families can all be worked with in similar ways. It is proposed in this section that there are different dynamics involved when counseling with the African American family.

Chapter 4 illustrates how the unconscious mind is programmed from early childhood by significant others and those not so significant. This programming subsequently directs the person's behavior. Before the person can change his behavior, after having repressed the unconscious elements that gave rise to that behavior, he must integrate the unconscious into the conscious level of awareness. By bringing negative unconscious material into the conscious level of awareness and working through the material, the person can begin to respond in a more positive way. This should provide a corrective emotional experience for those exposed to psychological trauma.

This chapter has meaning for anyone wanting to change their behavior and is not specifically significant for African Americans alone. The information is basic to any change in human behavior and could be significant for any group of people. The author prefers this approach to psychotherapy, and feels it is most useful in working with African Americans.

Also presented in this chapter is an idea of the process by which individuals develop pathology that is expressed later in their relationships with others. The main issues here are how we learn pathological behavior, and how we can utilize psychotherapy to help us cope with these problems once they become an issue.

Chapter 5 presents some basic research that relates to the relationship maintained between an African American therapist and both African American and white clients. This chapter points out that an African American client sometimes has difficulty with white, as well as an African American therapist; and that empathy, warmth, concern, and respect are key ingredients in a good therapeutic relationship. It is emphasized here that the problems which Black clients experience with psychotherapy are global.

Chapter 3

An Effective Counseling Model for Treating the African American

In conversation with counselors, it seems that many of them, both African American and white, still believe that there is no difference between the way you "treat" an African American family and a white family, or for that matter, any other kind of family. This does not seem to be any great revelation since most African American and white family counselors are educated from European and American perspectives, and tend to believe that "counseling-is-counseling"; and that most people, as well as families, have the same basic drives, motivations, and psychodynamics. It is questionable whether traditional approaches to treatment have a great deal of relevance to the African American experience—without some modifications. Some patterns that whites consider maladaptive may not be considered maladaptive in the African American culture. Family counselors

---

This chapter was reprinted from an article in Family Therapy, by the same title, Vol. 15(2), 1988, pp. 185-194. Only minor changes have been made. It was also presented at the annual Black Family Conference in Louisville, Kentucky in March 1988; and at the Annual Conference of the Association of Social and Behavioral Scientists, Inc. in March 1988.

boundaries in distinguishing between functional and dysfunctional systems in the African American family (Boyd-Franklin, 1984).

Any appropriate treatment model focusing on the African American family will need to incorporate aspects of culture thought to be basic to the adaptive functioning of the family. It is hypothesized that the foundation which family counseling is built, as it pertains to African American families, may be faulty (McAdoo, 1977). The many cultural dimensions of African American families are usually not fully considered when the family is engaged in counseling. Any appropriate family treatment model should clarify and demonstrate some understanding of values and behaviors considered essential to the understanding of behavioral dynamics found within the family; and, the total experience be taken into account. The technique used must consider the patient's ethnic group, culture, and race. "Therapists who understand and accept this theoretical position will have little difficulty modifying their techniques in ways that take into account such determinants of behavior" (Lyles & Carter, 1982, p. 1123).

Experience seems to indicate that African American clients have come from a different place and have many different ideas about counseling. The experience of slavery and subsequent treatment has impacted the family in such a way as to influence the dynamics that go on within the family structure. This, in effect, causes the African American family to behave differently from other groups and to manifest its pathology in different ways. With respect to this differentiation, there is a need to "treat" the African American family along slightly different lines than you would other groups.

When a counselor engages a family, more than likely the counselor will be dealing with a family system that is different from the counselor's own. The clinician has a value system, a cultural background, and a host of experiences, which will usually be different from the family being treated. It then becomes necessary for counselors to explore their own belief system, perceptions and prejudices. They also need to be aware of the cultural values of the family with whom they work (Boyd-Franklin, 1984). This is to imply that African American families are not homogeneous, but are as heterogeneous as the culture from which they live, and must be treated as such.

Inability to Afford Counseling and Motivation

Many African Americans have not been able to afford counseling, and thus, have not grown accustomed to being able to utilize it. The individual has mostly considered counseling a luxury and has been concerned with more concrete issues (food, clothing, shelter). African Americans have always relied on a network of kinships, friendships, relatives, and neighbors for help, as well as counseling and guidance; with very little reliance upon community agencies (McAdoo, 1977). The church and the extended family have always been important factors to consider when working with an African American family. This is seemingly true because of such factors as discrimination and racism, which caused them to tend to rely on a kin network rather than to trust outsiders. Counselors are usually considered outside this network and are, therefore, considered a threat to the confidential nature of their personal thoughts, feelings and troubles. The family may be unwilling to discuss personal issues until a relationship of trust has been developed (Boyd-Franklin, 1984). "While the white family may utilize a community institution, Blacks turn to their own family or extended family in time of crisis" (McAdoo, 1977, p. 77). In many cases, the family will find no resources to help with the family problem, and the resources that are available are not viewed as sympathetic to the minority experience.

<u>African Americans have a distrust for agencies.</u> It is true that bureaucracies in the past have had a very racist way of prying into the affairs of families while providing services. So, the family has become distrustful of agencies, feeling that the counselor is just another person prying into their "business." Another issue is that African Americans are generally forced to come in for counseling by one institution or another—therefore they resist. A family that is more aware of the purpose of counseling and comes on their own will likely be more motivated to come for the treatment sessions. The counselors must be active and extend themselves to acquaint the family with the therapeutic process (Boyd-Franklin, 1984). Confidence and trust must be earned; it is not automatically given (Sager & Braboy, 1970).

<u>Resistance of African American clients.</u> "Community services are often not utilized until a conflict occurs with an institution within the wider community, such as the police or the schools" (McAdoo, 1977, p. 77). If these clients are to be engaged, the counselor must clarify the role of the referring agency, and the role of the counselor. When referred by another agency, the family will usually resist because they are not actually volunteering to come because of a felt need, but are being forced to come. This, in itself, will cause the family to behave differently while engaging in counseling. Experience in counseling indicates that African Americans have difficulty with making an effort to physically come for counseling. Clients will say that they forgot about the session; had other urgent matters to address; say they didn't have the bus fare; that they didn't feel well; or, make many other excuses for missing the session. The main reason being poorly motivated for coming and being able to place a high value on the counseling relationship. It has been noted in the work of several authors how reluctant and resistive to treatment the African American client seems to be (Foley, 1975; Sager & Braboy, 1970; McAdoo, 1977; Boyd, 1977). The African American family has the same kind of resistances

that other families have, as well as the specific resistances peculiar to their own circumstances. It can be disastrous for the counselor to deny the suspicion, resistance, and hostility, and not take these factors into account (Boyd-Franklin, 1984).

> In a recent survey of family therapists (Boyd, 1977), 43 percent saw black families as more "resistive" to therapy than white families. Clinicians made such comments as: "Black families do not come in. It's harder to keep black families in therapy"; or, "Black families perceive the therapist as threatening or prying." Other clinicians felt that "Therapy is a new, unfamiliar experience for blacks. They are less willing to talk about their problems with outsiders" (p. 56).

Slavery Experience

The family was stable and highly adaptable in West Africa, before the arrival of other groups, where most slaves were taken from. After the long and torturous journey to America, on slave ships, the family had been divided, concurred and humiliated. They were further divided, separated, and humiliated after reaching the shores of the United States. The pre-slavery and slavery experience left the family with a constitution slightly different from most other groups. The male role was perverted and he was denied his role as father and protector. He then became sporadic and erratic in his family role. The female took the major responsibility for family, since the male was not allowed this role. This particular situation has caused some confusion in the family that has been passed on from generation to generation. Consequently, many males still seem reluctant to fulfill their role as husband and father. The female, in many cases, still bears the responsibility for nurturing the family (Green, 1975). She lost respect for the male in slavery that has not been regained, even today.

These kinds of issues still plague the African American family, and cause the need for them to deal with additional pathologies when compared to other groups. The female has taken a stance that she deserves all the amenities that society has to offer; but, the male has been slow or unable to provide these amenities. It then becomes hard for both the male and female to live up to each other's standards, creating an artificial schism. This puts them on two different levels and adds additional confusion to family relationships in present-day America.

> With slavery, black families were separated ergo—bonding and the extended family network was discouraged. In post-slavery society psychological scars were intensified. Racist practices continued to devalue personal worth and family pride. An example of this is the black male's relegation to positions of psychological and socioeconomic impotence in relation to his family. It must be remembered, furthermore, that in addition to the stresses of racism, black families must face the problems common to all American families (Lyles & Carter, 1982, p. 1120).

Traditional Stresses

The presence of racism, discrimination, and economic isolations, coupled with the lack of majority appreciation of culture and denigration of ethnic status, has combined to cause the African American family to have some problems that are different from other families. Through blending of African and American cultures over generations, the African American family has been able to develop lifestyles and family patterns that are similar but different, in many subtle ways, from other families (McAdoo, 1983). A large number of families have recently begun to show signs of stress from factors related to economic and geographic changes, regardless of race (McAdoo, 1977). African American families have the additional burden of having their ethnic group evaluated in a negative way; and, "While coping with the developmental crisis faced by all families, continuing pressures of institutional and personal racism bear heavily on them" (p. 77). In addition, the media has been a purveyor of false stereotypes as related to the family.

The Model

After reviewing the preceding factors and finding them to be pervasive with many counselors' experience in working with African American families, the following model seems to evolve as an effective one to do counseling with the family. The model developed is a modified version of the Jackson (1983) model, with some restructuring and other additions. It consists of educating the family about what to expect from counseling (one or two sessions), then educating them about the origin, development, and history of the family in America (two or three sessions), as well as pre-colonial Africa. At that point, a restructured Jackson model is used throughout the counseling process to fully integrate an orientation to counseling with a history of the experience in pre-slavery, slavery, and post-slavery; into the Jackson model. This model utilizes, in part a systems approach, drawing upon the entire community and its institutions. These things combined make for a unique treatment approach in working with the family.

In doing counseling in this manner, the family counselor truly becomes an educator, a director, an advocate, a problem solver, and a role model. This model should be utilized beginning with the initial interview. It emphasizes "wellness" or "normality" rather than psychopathology; group-centered behavior; strong kinship bonds; inherent feelings of cooperation and sharing; enhanced sensitivity to interpersonal issues, and an overarching religious orientation that provides structure, direction, and a philosophy of the interrelatedness of all things, as well as a comprehensive way of interpreting the universe and life.

All of these ideas are central to the African value system that has been passed on to the African American. Behaviors deviating from these norms are perceived by the community as an erosion of identity and cultural values (Jackson, 1983). The African value system sees deviation from the norm as loss of contact with cultural roots. Therefore, the model places emphasis on culture and community, along with the part that these factors play in the total "wellness" of the individual and family.

Proper orientation. In the first interview, since many families will not be accustomed to counseling and with what goes on in the counseling process, they will not know what to expect from counseling. This being the case, the family will need to be educated as to what to expect from counseling and what counseling is all about, while clarifying the counselor's role as well. This means that you as a counselor will need to explain your approach to counseling: what you consider counseling to be about, and what you will be trying to achieve while you are seeing them (Grevious, 1985).

There is a gap in the knowledge of the family concerning counseling, and some education is required before you can get on with counseling; otherwise, the family will tend to drop out of the session for lack of continuity of the client's and counselor's expectations. The family will need to have sufficient rationale for understanding themselves and treatment if they are to justify to themselves the need to stay in treatment. Sometimes, the client doesn't know what to expect from counseling, and finds the counseling process adverse to what they would normally do. Clients are normally not accustomed to revealing their personal troubles to a stranger; and therefore, feel uneasy and frustrated in doing so. This may be enough to cause the client to drop out of counseling for some un-clarified reason (Hines & Boyd-Franklin, 1982). The family will usually find counseling more compatible once they know the counselor is interested and that there is something to be gained by continuing.

Developing trust. There is a very important issue in counseling with the family, and the counselor is viewed as an authority figure dictating advice. The family has difficulty believing that the counselor's suggestions will be something that they should live by, since it is normally believed that the counselor's life is far different from their own family situation. Before counseling can be effective, the family must come to believe that the counselor can be trusted, and that recommendations are not tainted with values that are divorced from the reality of their own family situation.

Aside from these issues, African Americans in general, associate seeking assistance for emotional problems as being "crazy," and no self-respecting person wants to be thought of as "crazy" (Brannon, 1983). The male has more difficulty than the female with seeking assistance, because he correlates solving one's own problem with one's masculinity (1983). "Consequently, to seek help is synonymous with being less than a man!" (p. 170). These factors alone cause many couples who could benefit from therapy to not seek it.

Dealing with concrete issues. A large proportion of families have such extreme economic problems that you can't begin to do counseling until you have dealt with some of the more concrete issues (Foley, 1975). When a family comes in for counseling, it is not the emotional issues that finally bring them in, but the more concrete issues that cause such deprivation as to lead to a breakdown in the relationship that exist between members of the family. A counselor will need to address the concrete issues before any meaningful counseling can take place; and, in many cases, a family will discontinue counseling when the concrete issues have been dealt with. In many cases, the concrete issues will be the cause of the problem; the concrete issues will have caused a disturbance that led to the emotional difficulties. Not only will the client expect the counselor to very quickly get to and deal with the problem for which the client presented, but to do this within a certain number of sessions.

The client is not accustomed to long-term counseling and is certain to discontinue if it is felt that it is going to be a long "drawn-out" process. One approach is to contract for a specific number of sessions in order to resolve a specific set of issues. If, at the end of the contracted period the client feels that more time is necessary, the client can contract for more time. If the counseling ends and another crisis arise, it is understood they can return (Boyd-Franklin, 1984).

The middle phase. In the middle phase, the clients have to be constantly reminded of the purpose for which they are in counseling, and what is to be accomplished in the counseling process. The educational process that begins during the first and second interviews must be a continuous process of education concerning what counseling is all about. Also, in the middle phase of counseling there should be a continuation of attempts to modify the effects that pre-slavery and slavery has had on the family, as well as to help modify the effects of being exposed to years of discrimination and prejudice. All of these things have affected the way African Americans feel about each other as a result of developing hatred for others in the race and self-hatred, which affects our family relationships.

Counseling with the family should be an attempt to re-educate the unit as to more adaptive ways of functioning. This means that they need to understand the influences of pre-slavery and slavery, and how these things affected African American people as a whole. They must also learn to respect themselves and the opposite sex, to minimize materialism and understand how it affects the family, and to understand how economics help to further confuse the priorities of the family. The counselor needs to help the clients to be more aware of themselves as a group, to help develop a sense of identity and racial pride, and help them realize how the past affects the present behavior of families and individuals. The family needs to be helped to realize what must be done to get back on the road to a healthier family.

Jackson's Model

Jackson (1983) puts forth a model that suggests when seeing a client in counseling a number of things need to be considered: helping person, family, professional, culture, community, political and economic system, and the environment (See figure 1 and 2). This model includes, as part of the system, the individual, the family, friends, relatives, neighbors, the environment and institutions. Institutions are also a part of the system, since problems that occur between individuals and their environment produce stress. The model focuses on the whole system, but the primary units are the helping person and the client and family, since these are likely to be the initial components involved. It proposes the collective action of the professionals, of continuity of services, and of direct intervention within multiple systems. A service chain that encompasses the total network of the client is presented. In such a model, professionals from all spheres would be involved to help assure collective responsibility, and putting emphasis on change for all participants. Intervention strategies and assessments would utilize the client's

World View, cultural environment, and situational context. Interconnectedness of the system, culture, group identity, belonging, and reciprocal benefit is stressed. The emphasis becomes wholistic health and prevention rather than disease or psychopathology.

In this model, problems are multi-causational and require multiple approaches for solution. A comprehensive treatment approach that is broad in scope is utilized requiring a wide sense of responsibility for the client, the community, and for political and economic systems to which the client must relate. Systems, group focus, and networks are essential for treatment within this model. The helping professional must understand the problems that the client has developed as a result of functioning in the system, help the client to better understand the problem, and facilitate the client in such a manner as to help the client develop improved adaptive functioning involving multiple relationships within the system.

It is assumed in this model that the client needs to be grounded more fundamentally in culture, and closer approximation to African American culture is one of the goals of treatment. The model emphasizes growth and change in individual perception, behavior, and cognition as well as upon environmental structuring and change. It is felt that change results from assessing one's personal and cultural values. This model stresses the impact of all systematic factors on behavior. Change in any part of the system influences behavior and the quality of life in the other.

Cultural awareness and change. Social class, lifestyle and culture are all important to this model, emphasizing significant issues in the African American experience. The helping person in Jackson's model was to be an African American who was well grounded in African American culture. This model is being expanded upon to include a generic helping person. Such a person should be knowledgeable about African American culture and values, regardless of background. The generic helping person should also possess a sufficient level of awareness and

Counseling Model for Treating the Family

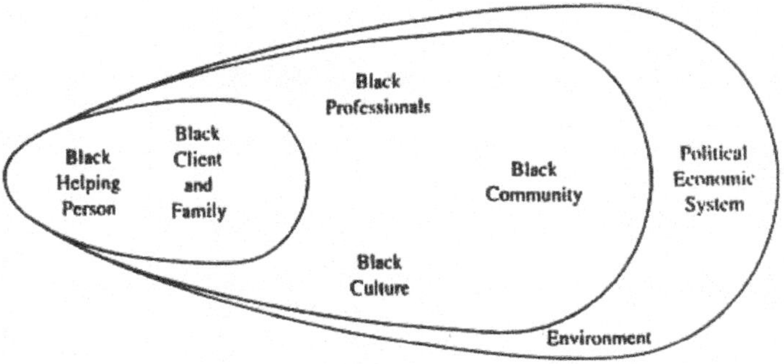

Figure 1. Proposed Black Clinical Practice Model (Jackson, 1983, p. 23).

Note. The diagram in Figure 1. and Figure 2. are from "A Theoretical Model for the Practice of Psychotherapy With Black Populations" By Anna M.Jackson, 1983, The Journal of Black Psychology, 10(1), p. 23. Copyright 1983 by The Journal of Black Psychology. Reprinted and adapted by permission.

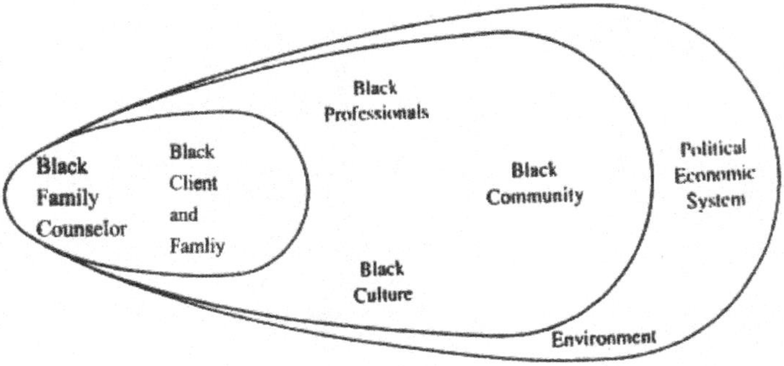

Figure 2. Proposed Restructured Black Treatment Model, Adapted from Diagram Above.

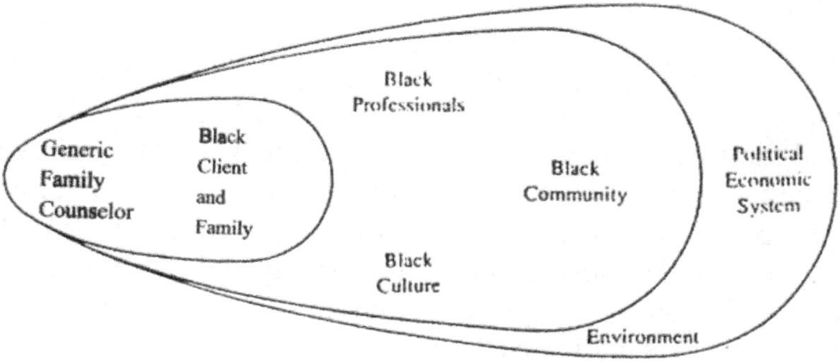

Figure 3. Proposed Restructured Generic Treatment Model, Adapted from Figure 1 and Figure 2.

be knowledgeable as to how these factors influence practice. It is felt that any helping person can be successful if he is empathetic, warm, concerned, and takes into account the individual's culture and values.

The counselor must work with the family to explore its immediate surroundings and involve significant others who may provide support, or challenge certain ways of interacting among family members, and pull the family to change. It is important that the counselor select only those members of the kinship network that are relevant to immediate or emerging therapeutic goals (Boyd-Franklin, 1984).

Developing adaptive functioning. An attempt is made in Jackson's model to develop a sense of groupness that the community has lost over time, history and sociopolitical circumstances. Race, identity, and culture are very important. These factors give a people a sense of uniqueness as individual members of a racial group. Synchrony of these factors may be viewed as helping to achieve adaptive functioning and optimal mental health. When the client operates well within the system, network, and environment, optimal adjustment can occur.

Helping person to family counselor, the generic helping person. The Jackson (1983) model is both an individual and family treatment model for the client. The family already occupies center stage on the model. The helping person can be replaced with the family counselor, and we have the making of a restructured model for working with the family, as opposed to simply helping the individual client (Figure 2). In Figure 3 it is indicated how the model can be further expanded to utilize a generic family counselor by simply changing the generic helping person to generic family counselor. This model is highly adaptable and flexible.

Summary

While people existing in the same culture do have some of the same motivations, perceptions, and psychodynamics, it is understood that African Americans have undergone a particularly unique experience in this country. They require a different approach to family counseling, one that will take into consideration the unique subculture of the individual, as well as the history of individuals, and the history of their ancestors. The proposed model is an eclectic model that takes into account the many diverse aspects of the African American culture, and provides a nutritive dynamic model for treating the family. This model takes into account the social, economic, and political factors that exist in the community and which cause African Americans to be resistive to counseling. The proper orientation, education, and consideration for culture are integrated in this model, and provide a unique way of doing therapy with the family.

References

Boyd-Franklin, N. (1984). Issues in family therapy with Black families. Clinical Psychologist, 37(2), 54-58.

Boyd, N. (1977). Black families in therapy: A study of clinicians' perceptions. Psychiatric Spectator, 41, 21-25.

Brannon, L. (1983). Marriage and family therapy with Black clients: Method and structure. In C. Obduho (Ed.), Black marriage and family therapy. Connecticut: Greenwood Press.

Foley, V. (1975). Family therapy with Black disadvantaged families: Some observations on roles, communications, and techniques. Journal of Marriage and Family Therapy, 1, 29-38.

Green, M.A. (1975). Impact of slavery on the Black family: Social, political, and economic. Journal of Afro-American Issues, 3(3&4), 343-356.

Grevious, C. (1985). The role of the family therapist with low-income Black families. Family Therapist, 12(2), 115-122.

Hines, P., & Boyd-Franklin, N. (1982). Black families. In M. McGoldrick, M.J. Pearce, & J. Giordano (Eds.), Ethnicity and family therapy. New York: Guilford Press.

Jackson, A.M. (1983). A theoretical model for the practice of psychotherapy with Black populations. The Journal of Black Psychology, 10(1), 19-27.

Lyles, M.R., & Carter, J.H. (1982). Myths and strengths of the Black family: A historical and sociological contribution to family therapy. Journal of the National Medical Association, 74(11), 1119-1123.

McAdoo, H. (1983). Stress absorbing systems in Black families. Family Relations, 31, 479-488.

McAdoo, H. (1977). Family therapy in the Black community. American Journal of Orthopsychiatry, 47(1), 75-79.

Sager, C., & Braboy, T. (1970). Black ghetto family in therapy: A laboratory experience. New York: Grove Press.

Chapter 4

Debugging and Reprogramming the Unconscious Mind Through Psychotherapy

Since we are living in a high-tech age, it seems appropriate to utilize computer concepts to help describe a way of doing psychotherapy. This approach to doing psychotherapy is not vastly different from some other techniques. What is considered to be different about this approach is the way in which these computer concepts and other terms are conceived, used, and applied to the process of doing psychotherapy. If a name must be given to this approach, the most appropriate label would be "programmatic psychotherapy." The way in which these concepts are conceived and used would seem to shed some light on the use of the unconscious mechanism in psychotherapy, and at the same time, demonstrate how one can be more productive in initiating and following through with the process of psychotherapy.

Individuals decide to seek psychotherapy either because they are in a state of psychological pain or someone tells them that their behavior is such that it indicates they need help. Eventually either they are sent for therapy or they come on their own. In either case the person is in a state of pain as manifested by his behavior, feelings, or sometimes both.

When the client reaches the therapist's door he is likely not aware of what the problem is or why he is in psychological pain. All he knows is that he hurts badly. Undergoing a brief amateurish analysis and informing the client what the problem is, as the therapist sees it, is unlikely to make a great impact therapeutically. This is because it takes more than that to replace the negative programming on the unconscious tape recorded in the person's head, which is causing this pain. By the very nature of the unconscious, one is not, and cannot be aware of what is stored there without in-depth analysis. Therefore, before the person can change his negative behavior while addressing the pain he feels, he must first become aware of what is on his unconscious mind (Joseph, 1979).

Part of the goal in psychotherapy then should be to help the client to make conscious what is stored on the unconscious (McEwen, 1983; Hein, 1974; Joseph, 1979) and to remove blocks and barriers which preclude the normal unfolding of developmental stages (Joseph, 1979). If you ask someone why he is displaying a complex set of behaviors, he could not tell you exactly why. If you were to figure out why the person behaves in a particular way and confront him with it, there is a good chance he would not believe you, because he really does not know whether or not what you have said is the truth. The person will not know what makes him behave as he does.

Since the client is not normally aware of what is on his unconscious mind, and believing that the unconscious mind directs one's behavior, it then becomes difficult for the client to speak about what lies beneath the surface to cause his behavior. The only way the patient or therapist can know about unconscious motivation is by looking at past behavior, simply talking to the client, or observing present behavior. The therapist then must examine the client's past and discuss present thoughts and feelings, in order to assist the client in connecting with the past and making the unconscious conscious.

What is proposed then is a way of doing psychotherapy by which the concept of the conscious and unconscious is central in the process. This approach utilizes three concepts from psychoanalysis that are also common to many other psychodynamic psychotherapies: (1) The concept of the conscious and unconscious, (2) The idea of using the history of the individual to interpret significant events to the client, and (3) An extensive period of time in which the actual process of psychotherapy is done.

The central idea is that experiences are stored in the unconscious as we mature and develop. This information later directs our behavior. It then stands to reason that when this programming has been the kind that would be productive of pathology, there needs to be a way to change the programming. Psychotherapy can be utilized to change this programming. Through psychotherapy, a way is proposed here to reprogram the unconscious and eliminate the pathological elements on the unconscious "tape," thus producing more positive behavior.

Early Programming of the Unconscious

Positive and negative programming. As children grow and develop, they collect all of their experiences and repress them into the unconscious mind. When negative, these early life experiences cause basic problems that must be worked through later in life (Joseph, 1979). These negative early life experiences are stored and not accessible to everyday thoughts and actions. The person is not aware of these experiences that have been repressed, yet they serve to direct his behavior (Titus, 1982).

At some point in the history of the individual, this programming has occurred. This repression of experiences is cumulative and circular. Each experience is added to the unconscious process, and as they are added, each new experience is integrated into the unconscious; the total of these experiences stand ready to direct the person's behavior at any given time. These experiences are considered circular because negative experiences produce negative perceptions, and negative perceptions produce negative experiences, resulting in negative behaviors. When the experiences that are collected and repressed into the unconscious serve to direct the person's behavior in a pathological way, the psychotherapist should be able to devise methods to reprogram the negative programming with more positive programming. Until more positive programming is added to substitute for the negative, the person will continue to respond with the same pathological behavior.

<u>The unconscious "tape."</u> Sometimes therapists refer to the unconscious and the collective thoughts stored there as the "tape," because it is considered that information is recorded on the unconscious much as it is on a tape recorder. The "tape" is simply all of a person's life experiences that are recorded on the unconscious mind collectively. If this analogy seems plausible, then the idea should be to figure out a way to get rid of the negative programming; that is, to replace portions of the "tape" that produce negative behaviors and record more positive elements so that behaviors will then become more positive.

The question then is how to replace the negative portions of this "tape" and record more positive elements in place of them. Other authors have talked about this unconscious process of recording information that results in an unconscious "tape," but not often about using this knowledge in a technique for what is referred to here as debugging the unconscious mind. Berne (1961, 1964, 1972) referred to this storing of information on the unconscious "tape" as resulting in a "script." The person then uses this "script" to direct different aspect of his life. This "script" is essentially the same thing as the unconscious "tape." Debugging in computer language means to get all the flaws out of a program, and then to rewrite it without the flaws. I have avoided using the term "erase" because there are always positive elements on the "tape," and one's "tape" can never be completely erased until death. It is only necessary to get rid of the negative parts and replace them with positive parts. This might be synonymous with "splicing" in the film industry: when a film is edited, the parts that are not wanted are simply cut out and the film reattached. Many psychotherapists utilize the concept of the unconscious. What is added here is the concept of "splicing," by which the "tape" is edited and positive elements used to replace the negative.

The Development of Negative and Positive Behaviors

Negative and positive behaviors are developed from the repression of negative and positive experiences that are stored earlier in the unconscious mind. When a person is the victim of negative experiences, he stores these experiences and later allows them to direct his behavior in negative ways. The same occurs with positive experiences. Often a person will say that his mind told him to do a particular thing, but he did not listen. The positive aspect of the unconscious directs a person to do the most appropriate thing. People sometimes say, "Your mind knows the right thing to do." If we want to improve our way of responding, we need only to get rid of this negative input that has been fed into the unconscious. Without this we are likely to continue experiencing pathological behavior.

Reprogramming the Unconscious by the Therapist

Prerequisites for reprogramming the unconscious "tape." First, the client must be completely honest and sincere about his feelings, thoughts, past and present behaviors related to each event. Otherwise, there can be no realism involved, which would make the whole therapeutic activity meaningless. If the client is not honest, there can be no realistic interpretations.

Second, before any meaningful intervention can take place, the therapist must have the trust of the client. If the client does not trust the therapist, the client will not believe that what the therapist is saying is representative of his thoughts and feelings.

The client must then admit that the problem is out of control, and that it is completely necessary for control to be regained over negative behaviors. Furthermore, methods and techniques must be developed to control attitudes and behaviors. The client must also consider whether he really wants to change, needs to change, or is happy the way he is.

The therapist's role. The therapist cannot truly solve the client's problems but can certainly help facilitate the client to solve the problem(s) (Hein, 1974). The person has been storing negative material into the unconscious since an early age, and it is very difficult to get this programming removed. One cannot do this in a day, and even with intensive psychotherapy it will usually take many sessions. The therapist's role should be the following: (1) To help the client realize what has been recorded on the unconscious "tape," (2) To help the client decide if he wants to do anything about the negative behaviors/programming, and (3) To show the client how he can alleviate the negative unconscious material from the "tape."

Wilfred Bion sums up the same stages this way—psychotherapy is a three-step process: (1) To understand the client by listening, (2) To communicate that knowledge back to the client, and (3) To help the client translate that knowledge into actual change, by working it through repeatedly in his daily life (Chessick, 1985).

The rest only takes time and constant effort. The job is essentially over once the client decides to commit to working for therapeutic change, but much work lies ahead. The person cannot simply become conscious of his behavior and feel that he can improve automatically, simply by being in the presence of a supportive therapist (Titus, 1982). The person must get the material in the unconscious to become integrated into the conscious processes. This is done by reviewing significant events and situations that led to the development of the pathological or undesirable behavior. It is essentially for this reason that clients do not change because they are unwilling to commit to hard work, and to make an effort to change

It is always easier to revert to doing what one has done in the past, especially when the person is constantly being reinforced to maintain the past-conditioned behavior. One is likely to continue to do what past programming dictates, unless an effort is made to change that programming. One way to change that programming is to get back to where the problem began and to refocus on the problem. This process is essentially one of reconditioning the unconscious mind.

Obtaining the developmental history. The therapist must go back into the childhood of the individual, or at least back to the "scene" of the original trauma, to help the person explore his behavior and see the unconscious factors involved. In this way the pathological behavior can become unnecessary as the person becomes more aware of the unconscious motivation for his behavior. This will usually involve exploring the developmental history, as well as the psycho-social history, to seek out and connect the person with the time and emotional situation where most of the unconscious material relating to the problem was implanted.

A complete history of the person is needed at the beginning of the therapeutic process. Once the therapist obtains the history and knows where the person is fixated, the person can be helped to progress toward changing negative behavior patterns. The therapist should also understand the present dynamics of the situation: present problems may be causing past issues to surface. Going back into some clients' histories causes a problem because they want immediate relief, as opposed to delving into their childhoods. Many clients who are "hurting" will resent a therapist who wants to go back to the "scene" of the original trauma in order to bring relief to the present situation. If the person has no idea of what kind of trauma may have caused the pathological behavior, the time from which he can remember, up to the present, must be explored.

The client must go back through family history to see why his parents were the way they were, why they did the things they did, and how it affected him. What did the person like most about his parents' behavior, and what did he not like? How could they have been better parents? How could he have been a better person for his parents? Significant relations and events with significant others, as well as those with the parents, must be explored. The client needs to examine past life experiences in an objective way and to see them for their positive and negative effects and influences.

The idea is that one must be realistic about these experiences before he can grow beyond them. He must view them in a positive way, though the experiences may have had a negative influence. The person must replace "I can't" with the idea that "I can"; "I am no good" with the idea that "I can achieve." The person needs to see all situations as experiences that must be learned from. By seeing things this way, the person can begin to generate positive attitudes that can set the stage for more positive behaviors.

Beyond the developmental history. Once a client has gone through his developmental history, he needs to admit that the past is over and he cannot change it, that his parents functioned the best way they knew how, and that all the people who hurt him were pathological and in part unable to be responsible for their behavior; but from now on he must get the necessary control of his behavior. Each significant event and relationship in the person's history should be explored for its value on his life. The negatives must be considered and positives used to replace the negatives. Each significant event must be considered for what it meant to the client, and how he felt the event significantly affected his life. How does the person presently feel about past situations? How does the person feel he can get rid of the negative behavior? The therapist will need to provide support by giving a realistic appraisal of these events as they are related by the patient.

Questioning the client is the way to make the unconscious conscious, and thus, put the client in touch with the problem. Sometimes the client will not know answers to the questions, and the therapist must continue to help the person focus on the problem by asking further questions. There are normally certain questions to ask, and the therapist must know which ones to ask to get the unconscious material into the conscious. The therapist's efforts should be to get the person to become conscious of the problems and behaviors underlying the pathology.

Connecting with past experiences. It is usually necessary to go back to that point in time where the person is fixated and to help connect the person with the past experiences which led to the development of the pathological behavior. By doing so, the person can eventually get beyond the behavior that is sustained by the negative developmental experiences. The person must understand the why of the behavior before they can get connected to the past experience in such a way as to bring about a change in his behavior. This is why the unconscious must be brought into conscious awareness.

The person who continues in his behavior has not developed an understanding of his past to be sufficiently connected with that past. Some individuals feel that they understand their problem but cannot change because only a superficial connection has been made. Understanding means more than simply realizing that an event took place in one's life, but also having worked through that issue and having mourned the pain and grief which gave birth to the problem in its developmental stages.

Modeling Positive Behavior for the Unconscious

Once the person is aware of the unconscious processes producing the behavior, it takes practice at trying to make the behavior better. The person must seek knowledge of how to gain control and practice gaining control on a daily basis until the negative behaviors become extinct. Without practice and effort, the person will sink back into the same behavior patterns (Chessick, 1985). Much of the work of psychopathology is accomplished in the efforts of the client while going about daily activities (McEwen, 1983).

The client should model after people who are seemingly in control of their behavior while coming to a complete understanding of one's past history: exactly who one is, where one is, and where one is going. One should always strive to be objective and not function from past negative input, making happiness a habit and realizing that one should focus on what is needed as opposed to what is wanted. The client should put himself in a position to start having more positive experiences, which will in turn regenerate and multiply, making them the basis of his behavior. Therapists should help the client to emancipate from crippling ideas, thus freeing himself for creative action (Hein, 1974).

Summary

The approach described is an appropriate way to provide a corrective emotional experience for someone who has been exposed to psychological trauma. The behavior therapy approach is a good second alternative for those that cannot commit the time and energy that this process requires, offering a solution that is too mechanistic, superficial, and quick for the author. For the client who resists dealing with the psychological trauma, from a historical point of view, behavior therapy would seem to be an appropriate method of treatment.

The "programmatic" approach described would seem to have a more permanent and profound effect. Other techniques of psychotherapy generally consider the unconscious in attempting to provide a corrective emotional experience for psychological trauma. However, it is thought that the approach to using the unconscious to provide this experience is conceived here in a rather unique and creative way. This approach seems to be more successful with those who accept psychotherapy as a traditional way of dealing with everyday problems. For those who are resistant to psychotherapy, they will unlikely be willing to invest the time or energy required to make this approach successful.

The author utilized this approach for many years in everyday practice.

References

Berne, E. (1972). What do you say after you say hello. New York: Grove Press, Inc.

Berne, E. (1964). Games people play. New York: Grove Press, Inc.

Berne, E. (1961). Transactional analysis in psychotherapy. New York: Grove Press, Inc.

Chessick, R.D. (1985). Psychoanalytic listening. American Journal of Psychotherapy, 39, 30-48.

Hein, G.W. (1974). Psychotherapy and the spiritual dimension of man. Psychotherapy and Psychosomatics, 24, 482-489.

Joseph, E. (1979). Comments on the therapeutic action of psychoanalysis. Journal of the American Psychoanalytic Association, 27, 71-79.

McEwen, J.D. (1983). The relationship of preconscious mentation to therapeutic advances. American Journal of Psychoanalysis, 43, 177-181.

Titus, M.A. (1982). Don't just do something, stand there: The role of action and will in psychotherapy. Bulletin of the Menninger Clinic, 46, 465-471.

Chapter 5

The Cross-Racial Therapeutic Relationship and Beyond

In examining the research literature on cross-racial psychotherapy, it was found that most of the studies examined white therapists/African American clients' relationships. In addition, reviews by Banks (1971), Gardner (1971), & Sattler (1970) reveal contradictory findings regarding cross-racial psychotherapy. Many of the accounts seem vague and inconsistent in their findings.

African Americans have been underrepresented in the role of therapist, and African American clients are beginning to question the services they receive from white therapists. With more African American therapists entering the field, the African American therapist is beginning to treat clients of all races (Griffith, 1977). African Americans are becoming more aware of the benefits of psychotherapy, and the number of African American therapists working with African American clients, as well as with white clients has increased. It is important to seek further understanding of how these cross-racial dyads relate to each other.

This chapter was presented, in part, to the Annual Meeting of the Association of Social and Behavioral Scientists, Inc., Jackson Mississippi, in March 1987.

We know that white therapists have always worked with African American clients, but an African American therapist working with a white client is a newer phenomenon. Racism has, for a long time, defined the character of African American and white relationships. There are many examples in psychotherapy that demonstrate some racist attitudes. There is no reason to believe that these perceptions are put aside in psychotherapy and would not lend themselves to premature termination when a cross-racial situation is involved.

Review of the Literature

Barriers in any cross-racial psychotherapeutic relationship. Some research has indicated that race and social class of the client and therapist, as well as training and background of the therapist, will affect the understanding and depth of the client's self exploration during a therapeutic session. It seems that white therapists have a better understanding of white clients, and African American therapists have a better understanding of African American clients (Bryson & Cody, 1973).

Nevertheless, Carkhuff (1971) emphasized the fact that effectiveness is not based on race but on the interpersonal skills of the therapist, as well as the quantity and quality of the client's responses. Training or a lack of it can be the most critical source determining the performance of the therapist in the helping relationship (Carkhuff, 1973). Racial homogeneity may be desirable for some therapeutic issues; however, it is clearly not a prerequisite for effective psychotherapy, as long as the therapist is sensitive to the conditions around which racial influences may develop (Griffith, 1977).

Barriers to the African American therapist/white client's relationship. The fact that African Americans are generally viewed as inferior by whites who consider themselves to be superior could cause inferiority/superiority feelings to surface and become a barrier between an African American therapist and a white client. The studies done in this area suggest that the race of the therapist influences the dynamics of the psychotherapy relationship (Griffith, 1977). Some white clients respond by dropping out of treatment prematurely. If they do continue in treatment, they may resist a therapeutic alliance, expressing anger by acting superior, challenging the therapist or assuming a patronizing stance (Jackson, 1973).

Barriers to the African American therapist/African American client's relationship. It is felt that African American therapists could use denial in such a way as to have negative feelings about their own identity, so that it becomes an issue for the relationship (Gardner, 1971). The point is that African American therapists might also experience some problems in working with African American clients either by over identification or lack of understanding. Thus, African American therapists must be prepared for many of the same tests that white therapists experience before being accepted as trustworthy persons (Gardner, 1971; Grier & Cobbs, 1971).

Present Study

This study is designed to test whether there was a differential premature termination rate when comparing a group of fifteen African American clients to a group of eighteen white clients. It considered length of time in therapy and whether the time in therapy is significantly different for these two groups who were being treated by an African American therapist. The assumption is that a significant difference between the two groups would mean that the African American and the white group had different premature termination rates. If there is no significance difference between them, the termination rates should be similar for both African American and white groups. The study also attempts to determine if, as a group, there is any significant difference between the mean numbers of sessions held by these groups. It is hypothesized that there will be no significant difference between the two groups.

Method

Setting. This research took place in a private child welfare, family service, and adoption agency in Chicago, Illinois. The part-time therapist provided services to clients of both a west suburban location and a south side location.

Subjects. The therapist was referred a total of fifty-one clients between November 1984 and December 1985. Eighteen clients did not appear for their appointments. Thirty-three clients were eventually treated in therapy: fifteen were African American and eighteen were white. Each of the thirty-three clients reported to the agency office for psychotherapy after having called with an identifiable problem. There was a wide range of ages and socioeconomic categories from all areas of the city. The services of the agency were available to anyone in need of therapy, regardless of ability to pay.

Procedure. Each client was seen and encouraged to return, if it was deemed necessary. The client continued with treatment for as long as both therapist and client felt necessary. At the beginning of the first and second sessions, the importance of therapy was discussed. The clients were continuously reminded of the importance of actively involving themselves in therapy. Sessions were held on schedule, and only race and the number of sessions for each client was recorded at the end of the fourteenth month. The number of sessions for each group was compared by race to see if there was a significant difference between the mean numbers of sessions.

Table 1

Independent Samples of Race

Group 1: RACE/African American Group 2: RACE/white

t-test for: Number of sessions

	Number Of cases	Mean	Standard Deviation	Standard Error
Group 1	15	6.6000	6.874	1.775
Group 2	18	5.4444	6.492	1.530

F Value	2-tail Prob.	T-Value	Degree of Freedom	2-Tail Prob.
1.12	.812	.50	.31	.624

Note: The t-test of two different groups (African American 15, white 18) with P<.05, showing the t-value with two-tailed probability. The t-test done for a number of sessions for both groups demonstrates no significant difference between the two groups.

Results

The white group had a mean of 5.4 sessions, and the African American group had a mean of 6.6 sessions. The t-test demonstrated that there was no significant difference between these two groups. African Americans clients had a slightly higher average number of sessions per client. For a pooled variance estimate with a two-tailed probability of .624 with 31 degree of freedom, there was a t-value of .50. According to this t-value, there is no significant difference between these two means at the $P<.05$ level of probability. (Refer to Table 1 for statistical information.) This analysis implies that there was no difference in termination rates of African American and white clients.

All clients who attended at least two sessions reported an improvement in their problems as reason for termination. Those who only attended a single session reported a change in perspective that related to a new direction or change in need for services. Of the thirty-three clients who had at least one session, eight African American and only four white clients did not return after the first session. One white and two African American clients did not return after the second session. Two African American clients did not return after the third session, whereas for the white clients, the fourth session was the next point after which three of them did not return. Those clients who remained after the third or fourth session would usually be consistent in their participation in therapy, whether African American or white.

Discussion

The original research question was: Is there a significant difference between the mean values of the two groups of clients who were treated by an African American psychotherapist, as measured by the t-test? It was hypothesized that there would be no significant difference between the mean values of the two groups. This was proven true by the t-test.

This study would seem to have limited significance for generalizing to other studies, since only two variables were used, with only one being used to measure the significant difference between the two groups. As a result of using a limited number of variables, some of the traditional controls were not in place which could impose some limitations upon the study. There was clearly no significant difference between the two mean values of the African American and white groups at the $P<.05$ level of probability.

Implications

It is suggested by this study that although superiority/inferiority issues may arise in the context of the African American therapist providing therapy to white clients, premature termination was not any more prevalent with white than African American clients. There are many factors involved in therapy with cross-racial dyads. It requires effort on the part of the therapist to engage most clients. The crucial question is not whether premature termination is more likely with cross-racial dyads, but under what conditions and in what way. It is suggested that to answer these questions, further studies are required in this area.

References

Banks, G. (1971). The effects of race on one-to-one helping interviews. Social Service Review, 45, 137-146.

Bryson, S., & Cody, J. (1973). Relationship of race and level of understanding between counselor and client. Journal of Counseling Psychotherapy, 20, 495-498.

Carkhuff, R.R. (1971). The development of human resources. New York: Holt, Rinehart and Winston.

Carkhuff, R.R. (1973). Black and white in helping. Professional Psychology, 3, 21.

Gardner, L.H. (1971). The therapeutic relationship under varying conditions of race. Psychotherapy: Theory, Research, and Practice, 8, 78-87.

Grier, W.H., & Cobbs, P.M. (1971). The Jesus bag. New York: McGraw-Hill.

Griffith, M.S. (1977). The influence of race on the psychotherapeutic relationship. Psychiatry, 40, 27-40.

Jackson, A.M. (1973). Psychotherapy factors associated with the race of the therapist. Psychotherapy: Theory, Research and Practice, 10, 273-277.

Sattler, J.M. (1970). Racial "experimenter effects" in experimentation, testing, interviewing and psychotherapy. Psychological Bulletin, 73, 137-160.

PART III

INTERNAL DYNAMICS

Preliminary Comments

It is important to understand the interaction of the dynamics in the African American male-female relationship, as well as some of the community dynamics that heavily impinge upon the African American male and female.

Chapter 6 points out that over the past ten years, the African American male-female relationship has become more problematic, conflicting, and destructive. It is hypothesized that these problems had their origin in slavery and have been passed on from generation to generation. These problematic relationships have evolved into the present condition of the African American family. We must rectify these conflictive situations if we are to witness the survival of the African American family into the future. Also, we must begin to study the process by which African American males and females relate from a conditioned process that is mostly unconscious. If African American males and females are to progress, they must stop blaming each other and realistically confront the problems in their relationships.

Chapter 7 introduces a new concept that has great significance for the African American community. This concept of "fortiscide" replaces the more unrepresentative and cumbersome phase of "victim-precipitated homicide." "Fortiscide" simply means when an individual provokes another individual by aggressive behavior to commit his own homicide. It is suggested that "fortiscide" is more characteristic of lower socioeconomic groups and, for that reason, has not drawn interest as a concept to be researched more intensively.

Society can no longer perpetuate the conditions that have led so many individuals to cause their own demise. "Fortiscide" is caused by similar conditions as suicide and is believed to be manifested by similar kinds of pathology. Therefore, further research into the concept is in order. It is only important here to discuss a very serious situation that occurs within the African American community and which seems to have implications for counseling with African Americans.

Chapter 8 discusses the recent explosion in the literature of ideas which would lead us to believe that African American men are in short supply. There are those who would refute this idea, but it seems clear that there is a problem with many African American women finding eligible men. Various reasons are suggested which support this idea. It seems that according to the way society has responded to the African American male, the shortage could have been predicted with a fair amount of accuracy. This scarcity is only a logical, calculable end result of a sociological process.

An all-out effort should be made to bring the African American male back into the mainstream of society, or it will be disastrous for the future of the African American family. Only after this is accomplished can the African male become more responsible to himself, his family, his community, and the rest of society.

Chapter 6

Some Destructive Elements in African American Male-Female Relationships

The Black male-female relationship had its origins when Black people first appeared in the "Garden of Eden"; but the greatest impact on the African American male-female relationship has come from slavery. There are those who claim that African American male-female relationships are problematic, conflictive, and destructive because of the attitude of the male. Some say it is because of the female, and others say it is because of the history of oppression that African American males and females have experienced collectively. The male-female relationship that we see today is probably caused by a mixture of all these factors.

Any way you look at it, the same scenario is obvious: African Americans developed certain attitudes as captives in this country. These attitudes that originated in slavery were passed on from generation to generation: poor self-concept, self-hatred, anti-unification, etc.; these deeply ingrained attitudes can be witnessed at the present time (Akbar, 1984). Akbar feels that, "Slavery is the modern genesis experience

---

This chapter was presented at the annual Black Family Conference, Louisville, Kentucky, in March 1989.

for Africans in the Western World. Contained in this genesis is much about the continued social, economic, political and cultural reality of African Americans" (p. l).

One should not underestimate the conditioning process and how characteristics conditioned in a people can be passed on from one generation to another. Some of these characteristics are conscious and some are unconscious: mistrust of each other, lack of respect for each other, and insecurity toward each other. It is very difficult to eradicate the conditioning process, especially when it is constantly reinforced on a daily basis. We can still observe the effects of the slavery experience five or six generations removed from the actual experience. We still carry the scars of the experience in both our social and mental lives (Akbar, 1984).

Clark (1972) argued that slavery, more than any other single factor or event, shaped the mentality of the modern-day African American. "Slavery should be viewed as a starting point for understanding the African American psyche, and not the end point" (Akbar, 1984, p. 8).

It is not the intention of this chapter to discuss African American male-female relationships from a historical point of view that goes back further than their captivity in America. This is not to say that some cultural elements that we see today were not residual from an earlier period in our history, but the major elements we see today were passed on from the era of captivity. Blacks around the world have experienced similar conditions as in America, and thus relate to each other in similar ways as African Americans.

The topic will be confined to the basic issues that seem to be at the "heart" of all the other problems in destructive male-female relationships which are unique to the African American experience. It will be worthwhile for policy makers and other African Americans to consider the ideas put forth in this chapter so that strategies can be improved which might be used to help the relationship of the African American male-female/family. An attempt will be made in this chapter to break away from the mainstream of ideas and present a rather unorthodox view. Though it is rather difficult to find supporting ideas for some of the views presented, and the ideas do lack a research base, they are valid based on empirical observation and study.

It has been noted that male-female relationships have been deteriorating (Gary, 1986). To understand this we must properly review the historical context and how it has produced these destructive elements. "There is something fundamentally wrong in the relationship between black men and black women" (Cazenaze, 1983, p. 341). Wallace (1978) contends that there has been continuous deterioration of relationships between men and women with increasing hatred and tension.

Relationship problems are quite common among all groupings of people due to changes within the society, but African Americans experience the unique problems noted above. If something is not done to change these relationships, further destruction of the male-female relationship will occur. It is important to understand why it happens and the role that destructiveness plays in male-female relationships.

The following are three important reasons why African Americans need to understand and get control of destructive patterns in their relationships: (1) Repeated destructive interactions can distort one's self-perceptions and thus damage the individual's self-esteem; (2) Destructive interactions reinforce stereotypes that inhibit the development of honesty and trust between males and females; and (3) The future of the family rests on the ability of couples to build strong, healthy relationships. African American individuals' strength lies in being able to love, be productive, and have unified families (Parker, Berieda & Sloan, 1984). History demonstrates, if we are willing to look, many ways in which the power structure has initiated situations that have placed handicaps in the path of the family.

The Destructive Elements

The destructive elements that are discussed here were derived from years of observation and experience. They consist of observations and feelings about the way many male-female relationships are constituted. An attempt will be made to put forth the most common destructive elements in the male-female relationship.

Part of the African American slavery experience is a feeling of inferiority. This feeling alone contributes to practically every aspect of African American behavior. Their self-hatred, low self-esteem, insecurity and rage are all outgrowths from feelings of inferiority. This experience was meant to inculcate a lack of self-respect and helplessness (Akbar, 1984). This sense of inferiority still affects us in many ways.

Mistrust and lack of respect. The male could not be responsive or responsible to his family during or shortly after slavery. This fact alone has left some negative feelings on the part of both the male and female. The man has existed in many situations that made it almost impossible for him to be viewed as a responsible self-respecting individual who was in control of the situation. "The powerlessness of the Negro man to protect his family for two and a half centuries under slavery has had crippling consequences for the relations of Negro men and women to this very day" (Billingsley, 1968, p. 61). The white captors insured that the man would be unable to maintain his dignity and self-respect because of the white captors' treatment. He could not defend or protect his family, and the family could be used in any way the captors felt would satisfy their whimsical desires. They could have sex with the captive's woman or abuse his children, both physically and mentally.

In reading Eldridge Cleaver's (1968) book *Soul on Ice*, it was understood how the woman would call to her man as she was being misused by the white captors, while he was afraid to answer or defend his woman for fear of his own life. It was destructive to male-female relationships as well as to the male's self-esteem not to be able to exercise this prerogative. This very phenomenon has had a devastating effect upon the relationship between the male and female that has lasted to modern times.

The female has not felt that she could rely on her man to protect her, and the male has felt that his woman has, in part, conspired with the white man to undo him. This dilemma has been understood by both males and females for a long time. How close can you get to a man than to cook his food, take care of his house, and bear his children? In this situation a certain amount of closeness and intimacy is bound to develop, giving the man the feeling that a conspiracy is in process. Some men will admit today that it would be hard to respect another man who would allow someone to beat his wife and kids, rape his wife, and sell the kids into service for the captors; especially when there were usually more captives on the plantation than captors. These kinds of issues have led the woman to question the manhood of her man. Though all were aware of this powerless situation, it had an effect on the minds of those involved. These feelings have generated a great deal of mistrust between males and females

The male was labeled in captivity as a "boy," and has largely been relegated to that role. Since the male's role in this society has been basically that of a "boy," the female has had difficulty seeing him as a man. There were slave revolts and many resistance movements, but none of sufficient force to take control of the situation. There were also a few individuals who tried to single-handedly right the wrong that was taking place. African Americans have always had a problem in massive unification, and the reason lies in the conditioning process after being brought to this country.

The woman's guide for what constitutes a man is considered to be an idealized white model. Since the woman has been confronted with the model of her man as less than a man, it remains difficult for her to see him as approximating the ideal white model of a man that she has been conditioned to respect and admire. This situation has affected her ability to trust or respect her man, and this is destructive to their relationship.

Insecurity. African American women have historically been given more opportunity in most organizations to both enter and be promoted than men. Cazenaze (1983, p. 342) says, "Some black men appear to be resentful that black women today seem to have more opportunities than they do," and this includes the opportunity of getting a degree. The woman has therefore made slightly more advances in society, both educationally and organizationally, than the man. As a result, the woman has come to expect more, in some cases, than the man can provide. Many single women are finding it easier to stay single and provide for themselves (Sellers, 1986).

This situation causes rifts between the family that filter over into the entire family situation. In short, oppression has given the male and female something to fight about. As a result of this process, men become jealous of their women when it seems as though they are pitted against each other. Consequently, men and women have tremendous difficulty in maintaining their family system. Women rise in organizations and in other positions while looking down on the man and calling him, in the vernacular of the white man, shiftless, lazy, and unmotivated; thus, not a real man. A person will naturally grow to feel insecure toward a mate who he or she cannot count on. This also has been a source of destructiveness for the male-female relationship.

Rage. Things that are done and said to African Americans individuals when they are young, as well as when older adults (discrimination, racism, prejudice, hatred, and hostility), build up over a period of time into rage. African Americans, as a group, have internalized a lot of conscious and unconscious rage because of their mistreatment over the years and have not had a release or vent for this rage except against each other (Grier & Cobbs, 1968).

> Studies by Smith and Gundlack indicate that conflict between Black couples often result from psychological problems precipitated by oppressive conditions. Problems of survival tend to generate situations whereby Black individuals become more psychologically and physically abusive toward their spouses than they would be in more conducive environments (Copeland, 1982, p. 15).

This built-up rage is destructive because it is turned on those closest to the person. Because of the conditioning process of African Americans, a destructive "tape" has been recorded in most individuals' head. We are all aware of how institutional racism has affected African Americans. They have usually realized that it was safer to vent their rage against each other than to express it toward the dominant group. The point here is that outside pressure causes individuals to more easily vent their rage on each other, since a person will displace their frustration on the most vulnerable source. The family or the person closest to the individual venting the rage is usually the one who receives this rage. African Americans in earlier periods would receive a much more extended sentence for crimes committed against a white person as opposed to those against another African American, thus reinforcing the concept of differential sentencing for African Americans and whites (Stewart & Scott, 1978). This also caused some individuals to have little qualms about committing crimes against another African American.

From earliest times in this country, African American mothers conditioned their sons to understand that it was dangerous to be aggressive against the dominant members of society; that they should obey, respect and admire the dictates of white society. The mothers did this because they were aware that very aggressive males generally ended up in jail, were killed, or became so frustrated that they needed psychiatric attention. White males who are exceptionally aggressive are generally considered good executive material for the corporation. There is, however, a difference between the way African Americans and whites express their aggression. Whites are able to find constructive channels for their aggression and energy; first is school and later in the organization. African American males are unable to do this for many reasons and, eventually, may become aggressive against person or property in some inappropriate way. This rage is then vented in many different ways, causing negativity in and destructiveness to the male-female relationship.

<u>Self-hatred</u>. Another element of negativity that results in destructive kinds of behavior comes from self-hatred. According to Alvin F. Poussaint, "Black self-hatred has been attributed to crime in the Black community, drug addiction, suicide, breakup of the Black family, and all other social ills of the Black community" (Burgest, 1980, p.149). "Blacks have learned to hate themselves, to see their qualities as unacceptable, and to see the qualities of white persons as the only ones that are acceptable. White is considered the epitome of that which is human; Blacks are not White and are

considered inhuman; therefore, Blacks who identify with being human first are associating humanness with whiteness" (Burgest, 1984, p. 182). This is why many African American men continue to prefer lighter-skinned women with almost straight hair, even in this enlightened age. We continue to judge our attractiveness by comparing ourselves to the qualities of an Anglo-Saxon. The more closely an African American woman or man approximates Anglo-Saxon qualities, the prettier or more handsome we consider them. This causes a lot of African Americans to stay in the beauty shop trying to keep their hair straight so they can be presentable. The persistent tendency to think of dark skin as unattractive, kinky hair as bad, and African features as less appealing than Caucasian features comes from a general feeling of inferiority (Akbar, 1984).

African American men and women spend fortunes on products and appointments to keep their hair either curled or relaxed. Many seem to have a fundamental hang-up about their hair, and for some reason they believe that their hair is bad and does not look presentable unless it is curled or relaxed, more like Anglo-Saxon hair (Akbar, 1984). If African Americans could start with this concept and take a look at their behavior, maybe they could begin to develop a sense of who they are and not need all kind of chemicals in their hair. Although this kind of knowledge, behavior, and understanding would most likely put a lot of hair-care product manufactures out of business. These hair-care product manufactures annually capitalize on the effect that African American individuals' hair has on their self-esteem. African Americans need to realize that hair is hair; all hair God made is good, and none is bad. It only matters that it is washed, cleaned, and brushed in some presentable fashion. All the chemicals to straighten and curl are a perversion of the way African American individuals' hair naturally grows.

How soon we forget what we learned in the sixties about the Afro hairdo: it was only a fad for most of us and we learned nothing about pride and self-esteem, as well as a feeling for what an African American identity is all about. It will take African Americans a long time to grasp this concept, because they have been so thoroughly and systematically conditioned. Many of them have unconsciously learned to hate all of their qualities, from their head to their toes. There is no sense in naming each quality—we know all of them. If you hate yourself, then you will hate and be destructive to everyone who comes close to you. It seems to be understood that a person has to love himself before he can love anyone else. This has been the whole point of the preceding discussion. Burgest (1973, p. 38) saw it this way:

> … many blacks hate their blackness and their culture because in the context in which they survive black is seen unfavorably and they identify with the racist conception of whiteness and the white culture. Physical destruction follows because in the African American's attempt to identify with the qualities attributed to whiteness they use every mechanism and device possible to destroy the existence of blackness. Evidence of this is seen in the high proportion of homicides perpetuated by blacks on blacks. The white system has succeeded in destroying blacks without overt participation in the act. In other words, blacks have been caught up in using a device created by whites for black self-destruction.

This scenario is very relevant to the African American male-female relationship, in that they begin to hate the qualities they see in each other and themselves, becoming destructive toward each other, both physically and mentally. One of these forms of destruction is the negativity and conflict seen in male-female relationships. The disproportionally high black-on-black homicide and crime rate is indicative of fundamental disrespect for African American life which grows out of feelings of inferiority (Akbar, 1984).

Games, Myths, Stereotypes, and Assumptions

Each of these elements are very important in their own right as contributors to the destructive process in male-female relationships, and they are all things that we impose upon each other's character. All of these elements can either be dramatized at the conscious or unconscious levels. They are more dangerous at the unconscious level because the one who is using them is not aware of the process by which the use of them is taking place. We play games with each other, buy into negative stereotypes and myths, and make erroneous assumptions about each other. Again, all of these are destructive to the development of positive and healthy interpersonal relationships between men and women.

We need to eradicate the use of all the issues underlying the negative concepts that we use and that have been implanted in our minds by the larger society. We hold a lot of erroneous assumptions, false beliefs, negative stereotypes and ideas about each other that have been generated through the larger society and that have no basis in reality. They interfere with the development of our relationships, and we need to dispel the myths and proceed to build our relationships. It is more important at this point to now relate the actual process by which men and women become destructive toward each other.

The concept "destructive elements" has been used to mean those things that can be seen as causing problems in male-female relationships. In the next section the term "destructive process" is used to mean the way in which the "destructive elements" become reality. It is useful to see the male-female relationship as elements and process because, in this way, it is demonstrated what the problem is and how it got to be that way.

The Destructive Process

Self-fulfilling prophecy. When an African American woman meets an African American man, there are generally built in clashes and conflicts. On the one hand, there are the feelings that he is not a man, that she can make him a man, and that he should be a man. On the other hand, she has her view of what she has been conditioned to believe about African American men, the historical dictates, the many examples of situations that indicate an African American man is not close to the model of what a real man should be. The problem is that most of these ideas exist at the unconscious level, and the person is not aware that she holds these beliefs and that these unconscious beliefs cause her to respond the way she does. According to Burgest and Bowers (1981):

> … the overriding assumption of what makes a good man in this American society is somehow tied into the definition of what a White man is. Consequently, Black men are measured by White standards as in terms of what it is to be a "good Black man" (p. 49).

At that point she has no other choice but to try and support her conditioning process and keep her feelings, as well as thoughts, consistent by trying to establish that he is not a real man—one that fits her idealized model of a man. Her attempt is to bring the self-fulfilling prophecy to fruition.

When the male meets a female, he sees someone who he has been told dominates in the family, "a Black castrating woman." This is not what he needs in a woman, and it destroys his feelings of being in control. Though he desires a companion, there is already a struggle brewing in his unconscious mind. The male begins to measure her against all of the glamorous white women he has seen paraded on television and the movies as the model of femininity. He then questions if what he has is the real thing, or if it is the best that he can have. Before long the man begins to downgrade his woman because he does not see her as meeting the standards of femininity held by white women.

The couple is programmed to be destructive from childhood, through all that they have seen and heard about other adults, and from what went on in their household. This is an unconscious process, and the mate unconsciously selects a person that fits the negative stereotypes which he or she has been taught to despise. This makes it certain that there will be problems in the relationship.

The unconscious process. By definition, anything unconscious is something that the person is not aware of, and yet, it serves to direct the person's behavior. The male and female unconsciously have doubts about their mate meeting the standards they have set for a mate. It would be inconsistent to believe that African American men in general are animals, yet to believe that the new man in her life fits the idealized model of a man. It would be inconsistent for the man to believe that his woman is the best that he can have when he sees what is put before him on television and the movies as the best there is.

There is then an attempt to maintain ego integrity by showing that their impressions are true and correct; that this person is indeed not worthy of their affections. To do this they must bring out the worst in each other. He must prove that she is not worthy of him, and she must prove that he is not what he should be. The relationship then becomes a battle, for if she has met a real man, she cannot let this inconsistency exist in her mind. She must prove that no matter how close he comes to this idealized model in her mind about what a real man is like, he falls short somewhere. He must prove to her that no matter how she straightens her hair, she is still not as feminine, genuine or supportive as the white woman he has heard about or is familiar with.

The battle then escalates. She attempts to make him aware of his shortcomings, and he retaliates, informing her of her failures and inadequacies. Competition brings out some of this destructive behavior, for there is a problem with who is going to take control of the relationship. She does not believe that she should allow less than a real man to take control of her life or rule in the household; yet she has been taught that the man should rule the household and has an unconscious desire for the man to be the leader. The man feels also that he is supposed to have this control.

There seems to be a general myth about the man being in control in the American family. The woman is usually in just as much control as the man. Although, in this culture the idea of the man being in complete control is a myth, there is still some unconscious conflict about who should be in control. Thus, there is a battle over who is in control, which can be a destructive battle. This situation is like two cannons pointing at each other with no possible winner, except to destroy everything in the immediate vicinity.

Bringing in the children. When the household is falling apart and the relationship is declining, if children are involved, they are brought into it. Each of the spouses communicate, in both an unconscious and a conscious way, to the children about spousal weakness. Chances are if children are brought into it, at this point they have been long aware that the relationship was on the decline. Mother and father both have done and said negative things to indicate how they feel about each other. The problem with bringing the children into this negativity is that it causes them to feel low in their own self-esteem and self-worth; if Mom and Dad are this way, then the children feel they must not be worth much.

When the children are older, they carry out this same unconscious tendency to be destructive in relationships as a learned response to what happened in their household. In both cases, male and female, they are simply carrying out the conditioning process, having been conditioned to respond this way. The male having been conditioned and reinforced to carry out the role of a "boy," the female is conditioned to see him this way.

Identification with the Aggressor

Identification with white captors. It has been noted around the world that oppressed people tend to identify with the oppressor. Females tended to identify with the white captors and to be critical, and yet help to enable the male to continue to function in a "boy" role. They urged the male to be passive in the face of opposition, and later denigrated him for having played such a role. A respect was lost then that continues to be lost until this very day.

The female tended to identify with the idea that the male needed to be "broken" and "trained," as well as humiliated, if necessary, to get him to make the necessary changes. This identification is evident today by the way the female relates to the male—not that she approved of this treatment during slavery. The identification was in the fact that the female began to feel that she must break and train the male, in order to ritualize him into manhood, just as the slave master made the male into what he wanted him to be. The man has a similar identification in that he tends to dehumanize the woman in his treatment of her, in the same or similar ways that the captors did.

The Only Real Man and Woman

In this society, the white man has been viewed as the one with the authority, the control, and the money; so he must be the real man. The white man is viewed as having all the power within society. He is the one everyone wants to be like. The white woman is also seen by the African American man as the idealized model of a woman, and he is slow to give the African American woman credit for being herself.

Thus if often happens that African American men idealize white women, and African American women idealize white men. Consequently, there is always something better, and what is available to them is not the idealized model. This will tend to leave one always searching and being dissatisfied and frustrated with what one has. This certainly causes African American men and women some destructive kinds of conflict, and is not good for healthy interpersonal relations.

Improving Relationships Among African American Men and Women

African Americans have been able to survive because they have been strong in the face of adversity and have had the will to struggle, overcome, and persevere. They continue to have a strong sense of survival, and many are extremely dedicated to their families. African Americans must be careful not to get caught up in the present-day myopia of society, feeling that everyone can do what is good for themselves only. In order to make the family strong, everyone must work to make it so.

Need for African American women to be more flexible. Women need to be more flexible in the future about their choice of a mate. One man on *Tony Brown's Journal* (1987) suggested that, "The Woman should not wait around for a man who has all the qualities she desire in a mate, instead of looking at a man with disdain because he does not meet her educational standards, or have all the necessary qualities. She must first accept him as a mate, if he is acceptable in other ways, and then help him to grow and become what she desires." Moreover, she should never try to force him into being what she wants him to be, if this is against his wishes.

<u>Need for trust and support</u>. We must learn to trust each other and provide mutual support. In years past, males and females worked close together to provide the necessary support and for the achievement of common goals. We need to go back to traditional norms that kept us strong and productive. Norment (1986) gathers these notes from the experts and emphasizes the following as being some necessary attitudinal changes: (1) To stop stereotyping each other, (2) To communicate more openly, (3) To develop a sense of respect and fair play, (4) To look beyond the superficial, and (5) To have realistic expectations. We must learn to provide emotional support, companionship, sharing and intimacy.

To improve the relationship between males and females, an improvement must be made in the family relationship. Respect, love, altruism, and a sense of togetherness must be developed. To improve our relationships, we must understand their historical development and go on to dispel the negative attitudes that serve to keep our families apart (Norment, 1986). Men and women must develop a healthy attitude for each other and for African American people in general. While the negatives are usually emphasized, we must keep in mind that a great number of African Americans are employed, have meaningful relationships and marriages, and that some are supportive of each other, both financially and emotionally (1986).

Set strong examples rather than walk away. Rather than walk away, we must learn to stay together and make an attempt to support the family. We must set strong examples for our children and work to eliminate the conditions which cause us to have these difficulties. All African American families should develop a survival plan for the whole family, which includes doing the following things: (1) Spending time together, (2) Developing an educational and social plan for our children, and (3) Being responsible to ourselves and our families. We must reestablish the role of the male in the family. The old idea of the man being the supreme leader is no longer functional. Women should learn to quit nagging and be more encouraging of the male to be a responsible leader (Williams, 1986). We need to break the old slavery method of teaching and training our young male children to be "boys," and train them through giving them a rite of passage into manhood, while making it clear that their behavior is expected to be that of a man.

Children must learn to respect both parents. Parents should not put each other down in front of the children. Men and women should encourage each other rather than engaging in conflict (Williams, 1986). We must learn not to play games with each other that give our children the impetus to go into relationships with hang-ups; the relationship between mother and father sets the tone for the whole family. Honesty and commitment must be the order of the day. Above all, we must realize that our problems are rooted in a traditionally racist society, where African Americans are not accorded equal opportunities.

Summary and Conclusions

It is very important that African Americans discontinue these destructive patterns and develop more authentic interpersonal relationships between males and females. It is important to understand the origins of these destructive impulses that are largely unconscious so that we can begin to deal with them. To deal with any problem we need to be able to understand the root cause of the problem. If we can begin to improve male-female relationships, then maybe we can do something about the present state of the family.

It is important that we begin to grasp the devastating effect that our history has had on us, and how we were conditioned to the extent that our past bears a heavy burden on us—even today. We need only to look at the history of any people to see how residual effects of the past tend to remain embodied in the cultural and mental processes of the people. We cannot continue to blame this destructiveness on each other, but must attribute it to where it belongs, that is, to years of conditioning and constant reinforcing of that conditioning. We should not have to wonder why we relate to each other the way we do, as men and women; the reason is self-evident.

In the meantime, we must keep in mind that many families are employed and have meaning in their relationships, and that some men and women are supportive of each other, both financially and emotionally. If each of us individually work hard to provide love and support for our families, we can begin to see an improvement in the relationship between males and females; thus, eliminating the "destructive elements" commonly found in their relationship.

References

Akbar, N. (1984). Chains and images of psychological slavery. New Jersey: New Mind Productions.

Billingsley, A. (1968). Black families in white America. New Jersey: Prentice-Hall, Inc.

Burgest, D.R. (1984). African/African-American relations: The binding links. The Western Journal of Black Studies, 8, 179-183.

Burgest, D.R. & Bowers, J. (1981). Black awareness and authentic Black-Black relations. In M. Asante & A. Vandi (Eds.), Contemporary Black thought: Alternative analysis in the social and behavioral sciences (p. 49). Beverly Hills, CA: Sage.

Burgest, D.R. (1973, September). The racist use of the English Language. The Black Scholar, 37-45.

Cazenaze, N.A. (1983). Black male-Black female relationship: The perception of 155 middle-class Black men. Family Relations, 32, 341-350.

Clark, C. (1972). Black studies or the study of Black people. In R. Jones (Ed.), Black Psychology (1st ed.) (pp. 7-8). New York: Harper & Row.

Cleaver, E. (1986). Soul on ice. New York: Dell Publishing Co., Inc.

Copeland, E.J. (1982). Oppressed conditions and the mental health needs of low income Black women: Barriers to services, strategies for change. Women and Therapy, 1, 13-26.

Gary, L.E. (1986). Predicting interpersonal conflict between men and women: The case of Black men. American Behavioral Scientist, 29, 636-646.

Grier, W.H., & Cobbs, P.M. (1968). Black rage. New York: Basic Books, Inc.

Norment, L. (1986, August). Resolve tension between Black men and women. Ebony, 153-156.

Parker, W.M., Breida, M., & Sloan, D. (1984, January). Exploring male-female relationships among Black college students: A survey. Journal on Non-White Concerns, 41-47.

Sellers, V. (1986, May 16). Dating game. The Wall Street Journal, 1, 16.

Stewart, J.B. & Scott, J.W. (1978). The institutional decimation of Black males. Western Journal of Black Studies, 2, 82-92.

Wallace, M. (1978). Black macho and the myth of the superwoman. New York: Warner Publishing Co.

Williams, R. (1986). They stole it but you must return it. New York: HEMA Publishing Co.

Chapter 7

Fortiscide: Victim-Precipitated Homicide in the African American Community

---

There has been a resurgence of reports in the media about individuals who have had some direct effect on causing another person to commit their own homicide; in other words, a victim-precipitated homicide. The concept of victim-precipitated homicide was introduced by Wolfgang in the late 1950s. The phrase is accurate but should be more concise and yet remain relevant as to what actually happens in such a situation.

The term "fortiscide" has been chosen to represent this behavior. Fortis, Latin for "force," and cide means "to kill"; combined, the concept means "to force another human being to kill." This new term should replace the old wording of victim-precipitated homicide. The meaning of "fortiscide" is when one person, by his own aggressive behavior, forces another person to kill him. The person commits suicide by causing his own death through an agent other than himself (Wolfgang, 1968).

It is implied here, as Seiden (1970) and Wolfgang (1968) have done that "fortiscide" is similar to suicide, actually being little more than a lower socioeconomic method of committing suicide. Suicide and "fortiscide," as aggressive impulses, are both found within the same individuals, simply being expressed differently according to socioeconomic and cultural circumstances.

In this type of situation, the victim cannot always be determined as weak, passive, and seeking to withdraw; the offender being characterized as brutal, strong, and aggressive in seeking out the victim. The victim in many criminal homicides is the precipitator. In this society, we usually tend to view the offender negatively and the victim positively (Wolfgang, 1968). Many persons who are killed in homicide cases are suicide-prone (1968).

The media has frequently discussed this kind of behavior, and some of these cases appear to be more like "fortiscide" than homicide. Such an incident which happened to a client will be discussed later in detail as a case example of "fortiscide." There seems to be a general renewal of society's interest in this type of behavior as reflected in the media, although there are few writings on the subject.

Review of the Literature

Very little has been written about this concept since Wolfgang in the late 1950s. After a careful review of the Sociological Abstracts, Psychological Abstracts, Social Science Citation Index, Criminal Justice Periodical Index, and the National Criminal Justice Reference Service, it was revealed that only a few articles had been written on the subject. Dequincy (1925) discussed some related concepts, and Garofalo (1914) discussed how victims may provoke other persons to kill them.

Several related terms and concepts were used to search the indexes, but after going back to the beginning of the indexes up to the present time, very few articles were revealed. The only concept that finally proved fruitful was that of victim-precipitated homicide. Most of these were articles or chapters written by Wolfgang, and he only wrote one major article with several spring-offs from that article.

One may wonder why this subject has not created much interest. There is possibly a lack of interest because lower socioeconomic groups are the major groups affected by this phenomenon. In attempting to arrive at a name for this concept, it was difficult because few agencies or police departments had a name for it as well. Though Wolfgang conceptualized this point of view many years ago, agencies and police departments referred to a victim-precipitated homicide as simply a homicide. The term "fortiscide" will be used hereafter when referring to this concept that means when one person forces another person to kill him.

Why a Person Commits "Fortiscide"

"Fortiscide" as a concept. "Fortiscide" means direct aggressive behavior, both physical and mental, which provokes another person into committing homicide. Wolfgang (1972) only talks about physical provocation in his definition of this concept. The victim will act in an aggressive way to instigate another person to kill him and, thereby become the cause of his own demise. The victim may deliberately start a fight, act aggressively toward a person with a gun, antagonize a person holding a knife, and has threatened to do bodily harm if he continues to act aggressively; or, become psychologically aggressive by mentally provoking a person.

The idea is that the person is in so much pain that, like the suicide victim, he is driven to create a situation to cause his own death. He either does not have the courage to kill himself or considers it more noble to die through this kind of ritual rather than kill himself. As an example of this, some Christians believe that it is sacrilegious to commit suicide. Therefore, if one is in enough pain, it might be easier to have someone other than oneself do the killing. This is not necessarily the main reason why some people choose "fortiscide" instead of suicide, but it is just an example of the kind of possible reasoning which could be used.

It is difficult to determine why some people choose to die this way, since there apparently has not been much interest in the subject to stimulate research. Lester (1972) suggests in his analysis of "Suicide in Ibsen's Plays" that shame, guilt, dependency, loss, and poor self-image cause suicide. It is suggested here that repressed rage, deprivation, despair, stress, hostility, the need to escape the pain of everyday life, and the experiences of being raised in a violent subculture cause one to commit "fortiscide."

Wolfgang (1957) suggest that, in many cases, the victim could just as easily have been the offender, since the victim would have killed the offender if the offender had not killed the victim first. In some cases, the victim has most of the characteristics of the offender. Another possibility could be where two potential offenders are confronted with a homicidal situation, and it is probably only by chance that results in one becoming the victim and the other the offender (Wolfgang, 1968).

<u>The mentality of the "fortiscide" victim.</u> The person who commits "fortiscide" has a particular mentality or specific psychological factors operating. There is little disagreement among behavioral scientists who attest to the fact that situations can be contrived in a manner which will influence people to engage in self-destructive behavior (Wright, 1984). There is also a psychology behind why certain people choose to die in this particular way rather than killing themselves. It appears, in such a case that a ceremonious execution is preferred over a regular suicide. For an individual

whose intent is self-destruction, suicide indicates defeat; whereas, "fortiscide" is considered to be a more active, dynamic, and masculine method (Wolfgang, 1968). Seiden (1970) suggests that, for the lower socioeconomic individual, suicide would be a confession of weakness and therefore the least desirable way of dying. Better to go down in an explosion in the world when you leave it, and preferable in the man himself" (p. 26).

Henry and Short (1954) postulate that the more an individual is externally restrained (the degree to which one's choices of behavior are limited by others), the more likely that individual will regard others as legitimate targets for aggression. Consequently, the lesser the degree of external restraint, while being frustrated from other sources, the more likely the individual will be to commit suicide instead of homicide. Although the victim who commits "fortiscide" is suicide-prone, he is unwilling to commit suicide (Wolfgang, 1968).

The lower socioeconomic individual is more likely to commit "fortiscide" because he is accustomed to aggressive, other-directed behavior. This individual directs his aggression against others who are considered to be the enemy and who have a legitimate claim of aggression against the victim. The victim will incite others to aggression, and therefore, assure an attack, since he knows that others in his environment possess the same values and are likely to react in an aggressive manner. Unfortunately, the victim will continue these aggressive acts until eventually one is fatal. Consequently, the victim destroys two people while obtaining some pity for his own death. In the case of suicide, less pity is offered, and no one else is directly involved (Wolfgang, 1968).

African Americans and "Fortiscide"

"Fortiscide" more prevalent among African Americans. Although "fortiscide" occurs throughout society, it is more prevalent among African Americans because more of them are in the lower socioeconomic category, and live in a more violent subculture. African Americans commit "fortiscide" against each other because they have never been trained to kill whites; therefore, it is outside their experience. Europeans have promoted the killing of African Americans, and since African Americans have been led to believe that they are part of the white system, they simply follow the practice (Wright, 1984).

It is noted that there is a belief in society that African Americans tend to be self-destructive (Valentine & Valentine, 1972). This is seemingly so because they are the largest consistently oppressed minority group. Whites in general have a higher rate of suicide than African Americans, but the African American male has the highest rate of homicide. African American males tend to reduce the suicide gap between African Americans and whites, if it could be said that "fortiscide" is closely related to suicide (Seiden, 1970), and is a manifestation of the same kind of pathology. African Americans are subjected to psychological attacks that deliberately prevent them from developing life-sustaining options and promoting conditions of self-destruction (Wright, 1984).

Suicide versus "fortiscide" in African American culture. Wolfgang (1972) suggests that African Americans commit a higher rate of "fortiscide" than any other group, while females in general are not likely to commit "fortiscide." Wolfgang (1957) also states that the male was more likely to be involved in "fortiscide" than regular homicide, according to a study done on homicide victims in Philadelphia. Again, "fortiscide" is similar to suicide, but the former is expressed through rage and aggression by those who find satisfaction in provoking someone else to cause their death, and is simply another method of committing suicide.

Seiden (1970) feels that there is enough evidence to state that young males believe that suicide is a soft, unmasculine kind of behavior. He feels that young ghetto males emphasize the importance of masculinity, courage, and toughness. Many of them are under so much pressure that they are bent on self-destruction, whether through drugs, alcohol, "fortiscide," or some of the other means of their ultimate demise. Under the present system, it is difficult to understand why more individuals do not engage in even more bizarre forms of self-destructive behavior.

Case Scenario

The following rather extensive case is presented as an example of one client's experience, in lieu of a greater number of shorter case examples. For the purpose of clearly defining the concept, this case is detailed to give an idea of what can happen when "fortiscide" occurs, exemplifying both mental and physical provocations. It is from the client's point of view, of which she has granted exclusive permission to represent, and will stand or fall on her truthfulness. No names have been used in order to protect the identities of those involved.

Wolfgang (1972) suggests that it is rare for a woman to kill another woman. Usually when a woman kills, the victim is most likely a man and more often her husband. Usually, "fortiscide" occurs between African American males, being more prominent in lower socioeconomic groups than middle or upper income groups. In fact, when a woman is killed, it is more likely by her husband or a close male companion.

This case example actually involved two young African American females and has simply presented itself at the appropriate time. It indicates how African Americans can sometimes act out their aggression and rage through "fortiscide." After the incident, the client was charged with homicide and began psychotherapy in an attempt to adjust to the overwhelming factors of the situation.

The beginning of the problem. The client began to have problems with the victim after the victim's husband decided to abandon her and become involved with the client. The victim chose to remain married to her husband, even though he no longer desired their relationship to continue. She began to harass the client by appearing wherever she expected her husband and the client to be together.

Next, the victim turned to destruction of personal property. She had someone steal her husband's car and break out the windows, as well as stripping the radio and gas cap. In fact, she broke the windows out of her husband's car twice on other occasions.

Then the victim began calling the client at home; sometimes she would talk, and other times she would hang up. She would call the client at exactly 6:10 every morning and continued to do so for a period of six months, insulting her and shouting obscenities. If another member of the family answered the phone, the victim would curse at them. She would often call all during the day at fifteen-minute intervals—sometimes talking, yet at other times not.

The victim continually appeared wherever the client and the victim's husband would be together and displayed irrational behavior, such as attempting to strike the client. Finally, her husband was provoked into fighting with her. She would go to his place of employment and get into fights with him that would end up outside in the street. Furthermore, the victim also threatened her husband with a knife several times.

In addition, the victim would sit outside in front of the client's home for hours at a time. If she happened to encounter the client somewhere, she would, if possible, step on her foot and proclaim it an accident. Once when the client was walking to her car, the victim tried to run her over, yelling, "Get out of the way!"

<u>The final event</u>. One morning, the victim called the client at 4:30, and the client told her not to call any more and hung up. The victim called back and said she would come over in a few minutes and demanded that her husband meet her out in front of the house. The client told the victim not to come, but within a few minutes, the victim arrived and proceeded to set off the alarm in her husband's car and blow her own car's horn.

The client put on her coat and took her gun outside to meet the victim. When the client approached the car, the victim asked, "Where is my husband?" She then struck at the client who, being pushed to her limit, struck back at her. As the victim reached for something under the seat the client grabbed her head and fatally shot her. This was classified as a homicide but could have been more accurately labeled as "fortiscide."

<u>Conclusion from the event.</u> The client endured extreme harassment and became so upset and furious that she felt she had no choice except to injure this woman and get her out of her life. The client was pregnant at the time and felt drained and exhausted from the experience; especially since she was working 12 hours a day and carrying a 15-hour load in school, as well as taking care of her daughter and trying to manage a singing career. At the time of the incident, the client was pushed well beyond her capacity to endure.

According to information provided by the client, the victim had been engaged in prostitution and drugs. She had no stable place to live and no steady job, with two children who were not being adequately cared for. The client felt that the victim had no respect for herself or anyone else; she lacked self-esteem and was despondent and depressed. From the information that the client received after the fact, the victim had never known real love and had been abused most of her life. She would have done anything to get some semblance of love, and was so possessed and obsessed with her husband that she would rather die than lose his love.

It is clear that this case represents what is being referred to in this article as "fortiscide." The client was driven to kill the victim through the victim's constant harassment. It is obvious that the victim used the client as a device for homicide, and that she desired this killing because of her pathological lifestyle and outlook for the future.

Summary and Conclusion

An attempt has been made here to introduce a more concise, representative term for the concept of victim-precipitated homicide. This term is "fortiscide" which means one individual being forced to kill another by the latter person's own provocation of an aggressive act. It can be concluded that "fortiscide" and homicide are very similar and are manifested by related pathology. Lower socioeconomic groups more often commit "fortiscide" because of their tendency to externalize their aggression. There is a particular kind of pathology involved in "fortiscide," and there is a definite need for more research in this area. Seiden (1970) suggests that our country might be in trouble if it continues to perpetuate the conditions which cause individuals to choose "fortiscide" as opposed to opting to live and be productive.

References

Dequincy, T., Bulwer, E., & Jerrold, D. (1925). On Murder considered as one of the fine arts, the art of cheating, swindling, and murder. New York: The Arnold Company.

Garofalo, B. (1914). Criminology. Boston: Little, Brown and Company.

Henry, A., & Short, J., Jr. (1954). Suicide and homicide. Glencoe, IL: Free Press.

Lester, D. (1972). Suicide in Ibsen's plays. Life-Threatening Behavior, 2 (1), 35-41.

Seiden, R. (1970). We're driving young Blacks to suicide. Psychology Today, 4 (3), 24-28.

Valentine, C., & Valentine, B. (1972). The man and the panthers. Politics & Society, 2, 3, 273-286.

Wolfgang, M. (1972). Sociological analysis of criminal homicide. In B.J. Cohen (Ed.), Crime in America (pp. 52-60). Itasca, IL: F.E. Peacock Publishers.

Wolfgang, M. (1968). Suicide by means of victim-precipitated homicide. In H.L. Resnik (Ed.), Suicidal behavior: Diagnosis and management (pp. 90-104). Boston: Little, Brown and Company.

Wolfgang, M. (1957). Victim-precipitated criminal homicide. The Journal of Criminal Law, Criminology and Political Science, 48 (1), 1-11.

Wright, B. (1984). The psychopathic racial personality. Chicago: Third World Press.

Chapter 8

Why African American Women Have Difficulty Finding Eligible African American Men

Enough has been said about the idea that there is not an adequate supply of eligible African American men to meet the marital and companionship needs of African American women. There is no need to further establish this idea, since it appears from the literature and the media that a problem presently exists, with headlines declaring "a shortage of African American males," "African American males in crisis," and "an endangered species." It seems clear that there is a shortage of eligible men with whom women can form and engage in "normal" family-life patterns. An explanation is needed as to why there is a shortage of men.

This chapter attempts to establish that there are specific reasons why men are in short supply, and that these reasons are historical as well as evolving out of present-day situations. First, the reasons why African American women have difficulties finding eligible African American men will be briefly introduced as a concept. Second, each of the areas of concern as to why there is a shortage of men will be elaborated upon. Finally, a summary of some of the implications of this shortage for the family will be discussed.

Since the phrase “eligible African American man” is used, it seems appropriate first to define what the author conceives as a “boy,” a “male,” and a “man.” A “boy” is a physiologically immature male in the process of developing, not yet having acquired the physical or mental characteristic of a “man.” A “male” can be either a “boy” or a “man” who has the physical characteristics of the masculine gender. A “man” is someone who has the physiological and mental characteristics of a male, has matured, and is ready to take on the responsibility of carrying out his role as denoted by society. In this sense then a physiologically mature male can still be considered a “boy” mentally. This is why the question is raised, “why African American women have difficulty finding eligible African American men”; it is to no one’s benefit for a physiologically mature male to be, in effect, a “boy.”

When the phrase “eligible African American man” is used, it refers to a single man with (1) a job, (2) a sense of purpose, (3) some hope for the future, and (4) a positive outlook to go along with that future. Most women look forward to getting married, raising a family, and building a future. In many cases today, African American women are unable to look forward to these prospects. The problem is profound and defies any single, simple, or cursory explanation; the reasons are inexhaustible as to why it is difficult to find eligible African American men.

The African American male has been miseducated by the Educational System, mishandled by the Criminal Justice System, and mistreated by the Social Welfare System. All the major institutions of the American society have failed to respond appropriately and effectively to his multiple needs and problems (Gibbs, 1988). African American men are now faced with some serious issues. This country’s policies have failed to eradicate poverty, and to equip these men with the education necessary for an advanced society. Society has failed to replace discriminatory barriers with equal opportunities.

The African American male is disfranchised as he grows up and never has a fighting chance. He is labeled pejoratively and is treated as such. He is frustrated, humiliated, rejected, and discriminated against on a daily basis as a youth to the extent that it is difficult for him to become a productive adult male. African American males have been the victim of many atrocities in this American society: legal executions, police brutality, violence, and ghetto homicide. They are portrayed in negative stereotypes: mostly as dysfunctional, dangerous, and deviant; as well as hostile, impulsive, dumb, deprived, and disturbed (Gibbs, 1988).

Only the most outstanding reasons why a shortage of eligible men exists are listed here. The immediate reasons seem to be the following: drugs and alcohol abuse, war, miseducation, unemployment, mental and general health problems, crime, imprisonment, homosexuality, and a preference for white women. It is difficult to assign priority of importance for these reasons; some may be more important than others, but they all have had a significant impact on the problem.

Most of the causes are interactive with each other. For example, if a male does not have a basic education, he has limited employment opportunities. This makes him vulnerable to stress which leads to mental health problems, drug abuse or other criminal activities. If he is born into poverty, chances are that he will not have the basic advantages of proper nutrition, adequate health care or socialization. All of these things affect his ability to function in school, and without a solid educational foundation, he will be doomed to failure. It is also a fact that even with an education, factors such as discrimination, prejudice, and racism, significantly reduce his life chances. This, coupled with life in a hostile environment—both within the ghetto and in society proper—makes it certain that there will be a definite struggle for survival.

Unemployment

Unemployment contributes to pathology. The African American unemployment rate rose sharply during the 1980s, and has continued to rise when compared to other groups. Much of this unemployment is due to discrimination and prejudice. High unemployment rates contribute to the high rates of poverty in the African American community, and are also associated with such problems as crime, drug abuse, suicide, and homicide. The African American youth has a very high unemployment rate. This is unfortunate because it is important to gain experience as a teenager, and those who do not will have difficulty finding work when older. Several different studies indicate that unemployment as a youth was associated with unemployment as an adult (Larson, 1988). "These young men will be poor marriage partners due to expected low earnings and unstable employment for years to come, contributing to the rise of female-headed households. Their low earnings will retard the development of the black community" (p. 123). Not having a job contributes to criminal behavior, drug abuse, and stifles the potential of the individual.

Unemployment and the "underclass culture" theory. Of African American men ages 20 to 24 who were not in school—those who should be just beginning their working careers—17 percent worked not at all during 1987, at least not in the regular economy. There seems to be a dispute over whether these men are structurally unemployed, meaning that the jobs in the modern economy increasingly require education and skills they do not have, or whether these men are products of an "underclass culture," where honest work is not valued because hustling, drug dealing, and theft pay better. When people lack even the minimal tools for employment, such as personality, courtesy, and elementary verbal skills, it is next to impossible to find work.

The latest evidence seems to favor the theory of the "underclass culture": even as the overall economy approaches full employment, and positions in fast-food restaurants and construction companies go unfilled, the African American unemployment rate remains in double digits, at 11.6 percent, and teenage rate hovers at 30 percent. These numbers do not count those not in the work force, those not looking for a job (Kondracke, 1989).

Unemployment contributes to instability. In the late 1960s, women entered the work force en masse, displacing many African American male workers. The stagnant economy of the 1970s and the shift to new technology and service jobs left African American men without the education and skills to compete for any except the most low-paying jobs. Today, unemployment among African American males is the key factor contributing to their instability (Poussaint, 1986).

The main reason for the deterioration of the family's stability is the impairment of the male's ability to control his economic situation. Lack of economic opportunity is the reason why many males shy away from marriage (Gibbs, 1988). More than three million African American men are unemployed, and the lines are getting longer (Levy, 1986). Dr. Robert Staples says that, "As much as 46 percent of the adult black male population is not in the labor force" (Norment, 1986, p. 154). In November 1987, 34 percent of African American youth were unemployed. Auletta noted that, if youths are unable to find jobs, they will be unable to develop work skills, attitudes, and habits that will help them to compete in a highly technological society as an adult. These young males who are discouraged will completely drop out of the job-seekers' market (Gibbs, 1988).

Female-headed households. According to the U.S. Census Bureau (1987), almost half of all African American youths under 18 lived in households that were considered below the poverty line, while two-thirds (67.1 percent) of those who lived in female-headed households were classified as poor. Forty-two percent of all African American youths lived in female-headed households. This kind of family situation has a negative impact on the economic status and opportunities for males, as well as females (Gibbs, 1988). "There is evidence that discriminatory labor practices and racial segregation continue to have an adverse economic impact on the black population, and are reducing the ability of young blacks to succeed in an economy that is switching from the production of goods to the production of services" (Larson, 1988, p. 98).

Drugs and Alcohol

Use of drugs and alcohol. Next to unemployment, the most disturbing problem facing the African American family's survival, and African Americans in general, is the massive abuse of illegal drugs that has reached alarming proportions in the community. Males are more crucially affected by drugs which sap their strength, both physically and mentally. Drugs are used for two purposes in the African American community: to dull the senses, which is mistaken for a sense of bliss, and as a vehicle to earn money. Since the larger community cuts off certain other economic and employment opportunities, many males rely on drugs to make them feel better about their situation, and also to earn their income. If an individual cannot function in a "normal" way, he can use these drugs to help him function better, that is, to anesthetize his feelings and eventually cause him not to feel.

The less drug involvement, the more productive. The less drug involvement, the more likely an individual is to attend school, complete high school, and aspire to higher educational levels. In short, the less involvement with drugs, the more likely he will be involved in constructive and productive behavior. Particular kinds of drug use are associated with criminal behavior and having spent some time in prison (Brunswick, 1988).

It is well known that drugs will destroy a stable family situation. Prolonged drug use will cause an individual to care only about nurturing his habit with no concern for others, whether that includes spouse, children, or other family members. Many males have become consumed by drugs and have become oblivious to all else around them. The use of drugs increases the likelihood that a homicide, suicide, or accident of some kind will occur in an individual's life (Brunswick, 1988). In addition, the use of drugs is usually associated with dropping out of school, mental or physical health problems, unemployment, and having spent some time in prison. All of these are deleterious to and incongruent with family life.

Physical and Mental Health

Deprivation and neglect. African American males are the victims of the cumulative effects of neglect of their physical and mental health needs. They are born, in many cases, out of wedlock to young teenage mothers and into low-income families, with the disadvantages of being African American, poor, and illegitimate. Moreover, their mothers are likely to have experienced prenatal, perinatal, and postnatal problems associated with pregnancy. Many of these children are born prematurely with low birth weight, and subsequently receive poor nutrition and a lack of vitamin supplement in their diet. These unmarried mothers usually have poor maternal or child-rearing skills and cannot support the child emotionally or financially. Many of these mothers abuse, neglect, or reject their children. Their offspring are more likely to experience long-term negative outcome in health, education and income. Environmental problems make these children vulnerable to many other problems (Gibbs, 1988). In addition, these children receive poor medical care, and grow up without basic requirements for a healthy mind and body (1988).

Behavioral risk. There is a close relationship between physical and mental health in the African American community. The conditions associated with poverty and discrimination (poor nutrition, substandard housing, lack of adequate health care) are exacerbated by behavioral risk associated with the subculture of the inner city (delinquency, substance abuse, family and community violence). These individuals increase their risk of physical and mental health problems by exposure to and involvement in self-destructive behavioral patterns which makes them vulnerable to psychiatric disorders, venereal disease, drug addiction, and physical disabilities (Gibbs, 1988).

Oppressor and oppressed. African American men have a higher rate of severe mental disorder than African American women. A number of studies report that many more males than females feel a lack of control and power over their environment. Males "give up" more easily and assume the "victim's" role (Poussaint, 1986). Of course, there is a reason for males to perceive the situation as useless and to give up. The white society sees the African American males as its greatest rivals, and makes every effort to neutralize them. Concerted efforts are mounted to push them out of the economic sector and put them in prison, as well as to deny them educational opportunities. Innis says that this is partly the result of a natural biological process, where conflict between the male members of all animal species is greater than between females (Hatchett, 1986). In a society where you have the oppressed and the oppressor, says Poussaint, "I think that the oppression is primarily directed toward the male" (Jones, 1986, p. 19).

Difficulty negotiating the system. African American men experience a sense of isolation and a lack of purpose, with difficulty and frustration in negotiating the system; thus, they become violent and angry. They are full of rage, volatile, explosive, and dangerous because of barriers that prevent them from negotiating the system. Instead of harnessing this energy in a constructive manner to fight the system, they take out their frustration on each other, their neighbors, and their families.

Education

Need for an education. If the African American male is to advance himself within the society where he must grow and develop, it is a prerequisite that he acquire the necessary education which would lead to that advancement. If the ability to get an education is thwarted, then the chances of maximizing his opportunities are adversely affected. Education alone will not make or break the African American male, but will significantly affect his life chances to open certain political, social, and economic doors. Education is the initial preparation that helps an individual to live productively in society. Therefore, the African American male seems destined to failure, since the educational system is failing to adequately prepare him for survival in an increasingly informational and technological society.

Low educational achievement. The African American male achieves less education, with fewer of them graduating from either high school or college, than any other group of individuals. He is constantly placed in low-performance groups at the beginning of his high school years, and is likely to continue in low-ability tracks. Expectations of him are low, and thus, his performance becomes equal to what is expected. More males drop out of school at all levels than any other group. African Americans, taken as a whole, are the lowest in all categories, and males are lower than females in all categories mentioned (Reed, 1988). There are 769,000 women ages 25 to 54 with four years or more of college, but only 633,000 men in this age group with comparable education (Norment, 1986). The male's culture is in conflict with the values of the educational system. This originates with male child-rearing practices (Hatchett, 1986).

Need for constant nurturing and reinforcement. African American males enter the school system to be put on the shelves and ignored; urban schools are particular cold and un-giving to our male children. Dr. Lyle says, "They are viewed as a nuisance and receive all kinds of unfair labels such as hyperactive or slow learner, which haunts them for the balance of their primary education" (Jones, 1986, p. 19). Wright (1984) feels that instead of labeling the child as having a learning disability, teachers of preschool and elementary school age children should give more attention to perceptual development: rather than to subjects such as reading, arithmetic, or science, since many children have difficulties with this type of learning early in their school experience.

Dr. Lyle further says that Jawanza Kunjufu has termed this devastation that many males experience in elementary school as, "the fourth grade failure syndrome" (Jones, 1986). If young males do not receive constant reinforcement and nurturing at this point, they could become adults who are politically and socially impotent. Dr. Lyle says that, "The young black male is a very active person, and some people attach a negative nomenclature to that activity" (p. 19). Males have a high dropout rate from high school and fail to complete college. A high percentage of males who leave school do so for disciplinary reasons; males have more problems with discipline than any other group. It is important to know an individual's preferred modality of learning, whether sensory, visual or hearing. Once this is determined, the teacher can cater the lesson to the particular student (Wright, 1984).

African American women fit better into the educational system. The inimical white middle-class value system of the classroom causes problems for African American males. Females more easily fit into the educational structure, and are more encouraged to get an education. "According to census data and demographic studies by Black scholars, at the college level, 60 percent of the total enrollment of Black students and 70-80 percent of those who graduate are women. Males generally respond to challenging, personal, and social situations in an individualistic, aggressive manner. Females are taught to be more passive, and to conform to the system" (Hatchett, 1986, p. 36). In our large cities 60 to 70 percent of males drop out of high school (Poussaint, 1986). Males are not entering the professions as rapidly as women (Hatchett, 1986). According to the 1980 census, women did better than men in all professional categories (Jones, 1986). This contributes to one of the most frequently heard complaints, that many African American women have difficulties finding an African American man on their level.

The need for more basic skills training. The African American high school dropout rate decreased from 23.8 percent in 1960 to 13.2 percent in 1984. Nevertheless, many African American high school students remain functionally illiterate. The 1981 census data indicated that 21 percent of all males between ages 18 and 19, and 25 percent of all males between ages 20 and 21, had neither completed nor were presently enrolled in high school in 1980. More than one in five males of the 18 to 21 age group do not have a basic certificate or basic skills which are prerequisite in our society for most entry-level jobs, apprenticeship programs, military service, or post secondary education (Gibbs, 1988). The educational system is not serving the African American male, and it should be easy to understand how his chances of being productive have been limited. The fact that he is not being appropriately educated is the very reason why he will eventually be inaccessible to the female and nonfunctional within a family context.

Prison and Crime

Large numbers of African Americans are killed by violent crimes. Fifty-one percent of violent crimes in America are committed by African Americans. One out of every six African Americans will be arrested by the age of 19. Twenty-five percent of the income of African American youth comes from crime. One out of every 133 Americans will be killed by violent crimes, including one out of every 369 white American females; one out of every 104 African American females; and one out of every 22 African American men. African American men run the highest risk of losing their lives to violent crimes. Forty-five percent of Americans arrested for murder are African Americans; 41 percent are under age 28. Ninety-four percent of African American murder victims are slain by other African Americans (Riley, 1986).

Early indoctrination of African American males. There is an over representation of African American males in the criminal justice system. There are many social problems in the community which predispose the male towards criminal activity. Because of these problems, many males become indoctrinated with the criminal justice system early in their development. Once an individual becomes a part of this system, it is likely that he will continue to be involved throughout his life. It is well known that more males are in the system than females. African American males are more likely to be delinquent, to be involved in violent and other serious crimes than other groups (Dembo, 1988).

A quarter of a million African American males are incarcerated in prison. African Americans constitute 12 percent of the U.S. population, but they made up 46 percent of the inmates in U.S. prisons in 1985, and 60 percent of those arrested for murder in U.S. cities in 1987 (Kondracke, 1989). It has been estimated that on any given day the state prison population contains more than five percent of all African American males in their 20s. It is also predicted that up to 15 percent of all African American males will spend some time in an adult prison, while only two to three percent of whites will do so (Krisberg et al., 1986). Statistics in 1989 estimated that 60 percent of those in prison were African American, and that by the turn of the century 70 percent of African American males will be or will have been in prison.

This disproportionate involvement in the criminal justice system results in severe limitations on their educational and occupational opportunities; creating a vicious cycle of delinquency, incarceration, recidivism, chronic criminal careers, unemployment, and marginal social adaptation in adulthood (Tolmach, 1985). African Americans are more likely to be arrested, charged, convicted, as well as serve time for an offense (Dembo, 1988).

Homicides, Suicides and Accidents

Accidents. The second leading cause of death among young African American males is accidents, often as a result of growing up around unsafe conditions such as broken windows, missing stairs, falling plaster, defective elevators, dangerous playground equipment, rat infested, and other generally unsafe environmental conditions. There are more males born than females, but more male babies die. Men have a lower life expectancy, and many die at a young age from homicides, suicides, and accidents. Nearly 2,000 youth die or are severely disabled in accidents and injuries every year (Gibbs, 1988). In addition, boys have a higher mortality rate than girls (1988).

Because of the situations that are related to accidents, there are only 89 African American males for every 100 females. One social scientist estimates that there is only one available male per five unmarried females (Poussaint, 1986). In 1980 there were 1,278,414 more females of marriageable age than there were available males; including single, widowed and divorced (Jones, 1986).

Suicide. In the not too distant past, suicide in the African American community was virtually nonexistent. In fact, in considering all possibilities of life and death, suicide for African Americans was not an option (Wright, 1984). African American suicide is a method of genocide which is being promoted and controlled worldwide by the white race. Consequently, there is no such phenomenon as "African American suicide" when suicide is defined as the willful and deliberate act of taking one's own life (1984).

African Americans are being programmed for self-destruction, for political reasons, and suicide is one of the end results. Wright called this concept "mentacide" (1984) "Which he defined as the deliberate and systematic destruction of a group's mind with the purpose of extirpation of the group."

Suicide is now one of the leading causes of death among African American males; the third leading cause of death among African American youths. In the National Urban League's publication, *Running the Gauntlet: African American Men in America*, author James McGhee notes that males commit suicide, when they have most of their lives yet to live. Males perhaps, realize at a young age that they may never control their destinies (Jones, 1986). The suicide rate for males has tripled since 1960. At a time when males should be developing an identity, pursuing a career, or starting a family, many of them are destroying themselves (Gibbs, 1988). With the loss of support from major institutions within the African American community—strong family, church, fraternal and social organizations, community school, and extended kin and support networks—there has been a loss of shared values, a sense of social cohesion, and mutual support; all of which in the past promoted a low suicide rate.

Homicide. Homicide is currently the leading cause of death among young African American males (15 to 24 years old). "The 1982 homicide rate for this group was 72.0 per 100,000 population, nearly six times the rate for white males in the same age range" (Dembo, 1988, p. 138). In 1977, more young African American men (5,734) died from homicide than were killed from 1963 to 1972 in the Vietnam War (5,640). Young males kill each other over drugs, women, money, or simply to avenge a real or imaginary insult (Gibbs, 1988).

African American males kill each other much more frequently than white males. This is caused by high levels of stress, depression, social pathology, and is contributed to by such factors as high levels of crime, violence, and social disorganization; excessive crowding; social isolation from mainstream society. These things generate feelings of powerlessness, despair, and social alienation.

Other Reasons Why African American Men Are Unavailable to Their Women

Vietnam War. We know that many African America men died in the Vietnam War, without quoting exact numbers. Previously, it was stated that between 1963 and 1972, 5,640 African Americans died in the Vietnam War. These figures may not be exact but give us some idea, since we recognize the difficulty in obtaining accurate statistics. Remember that this figure covers only the years between 1963 and 1972, and the war did not end until 1977. It has been stated that African American men died disproportionally to their numbers in the population. This left many women without their men, and decreased the supply of men available to women in general.

Homosexuality. As with all groups, a percentage of African American males are homosexual. It is not felt that homosexuality is disproportionally represented among African American males, but is simply an ever-present factor. This also decreased the supply of available men.

Preference for white women. A certain percentage of African American males prefer white women, and there are complex reasons why this is so. Some suggest that the reason is one of deprivation, and others believe it is because opposites attract; there are many other reasons discussed as well.

Working Toward a Solution

The question then becomes: What can be done to improve the condition of a shortage of African American males? Some of the suggestions below will indirectly, while others will directly, help to improve the male shortage.

(1) Bring males and females into the mainstream of society. End racial discrimination in economic, social, and political sectors. Improve the overall quality of life.

(2) Get control of self, family, money, schools, neighborhoods, and communities.

(3) Establish a public policy designed to preserve the African American family.

(4) Establish a public policy designed to develop and provide jobs. This includes training programs and more money for student loans, as well as loans and grants for higher education. Equal job opportunities should also be provided.

(5) Males need to receive the kind of training that would fortify them against racial prejudice, if this is possible. Every individual should become thoroughly knowledgeable about history—both American and world history.

(6) Attain or develop an economic base so that African Americans will not need to be dependent on others for resources and job opportunities. This includes developing networks among one another so that attaining success is not as difficult as it would ordinarily be. This means a program of buying from African Americans, which could help them to become economically self-sufficient.

(7) Parents should try to serve as better role models for their children. They should be more caring and concerned about their children. Parents must work harder at motivating children to do well at whatever they do. There also should be more African Americans serving as role models in the schools—especially men.

(8) A more equitable system of justice should be established in the courts, as well as politically and socially.

(9) Men must spend more time teaching their sons about the realities of society, and how they can insulate themselves against bigotry to make for a better adjustment. Programs need to be set up to promote the identity, self-worth, and self-esteem of both youth and adults.

(10) The community should establish training institutions for young males, as well as programs to train adults—first! There should be more responsiveness to the males from the community.

(11) Develop a higher quality and quantity of head start and developmental education programs for lower-income individuals. There should be nutrition programs for lower-income families, as well as better living environments.

(12) Focus on motivation to work together with other African Americans to eliminate self-hate and self-destruction. Develop better relationships between men and women.

(13) Discontinue the attempts of the larger society to emasculate and disfranchise males. Rally the institutions in the community, such as churches, to come to the aid of the male and his family. Efforts should be made to keep the family intact, and it must become the basic concern of everyone. Programs should be set up to prevent teen pregnancies.

(14) We must become less concerned with materialism and more concerned with authentic relationships.

(15) Development of an excellent school system: elementary, secondary, and college. If the above things are accomplished, it will not be as difficult to motivate young men to pursue goals of higher education.

Summary.

The destruction of the African American male is the most distressing problem facing the family. He is being destroyed by street crime, drug addiction, and other anti-social behavior, ultimately ending up in jail, a mental institution, on drugs, or dead. If he does not get caught in any of these traps, he is still rendered useless to African American women because he either becomes homosexual or prefers white women. Something must be done to remove the social, educational, economic, and political barriers, as well as social processes which cause the destruction of the male.

The condition of the male is due to many complex factors; there is no simple answer. He is likely to be born to an unwed teenage mother who had limited education and other limited choices. To suffer all the conditions of poverty, including unstable family life and poor health, and then to be exposed to discrimination, prejudice and racism or other major factors that contribute to his condition. The hostile elements that he is forced to face almost insure that he will not survive. If he does survive, he is crippled to the extent of being nonfunctional as a companion or provider for the female.

The male will face annihilation if something is not done, but at what cost to the rest of society? Must we go on building bigger and better prisons to hold these individuals, where they will ultimately end up, or after destroying these lives, to warehouse them in mental institutions or jails for brief periods, only to be returned to the streets? The ultimate solution is to develop preventive and remedial programs that will enable these individuals to participate in the mainstream society. But we do need preventive programs to help young males not to have to go through these problems.

In recent years, society has not improved in its discriminatory practices, and has had to build bigger and better locks and more advanced security systems. If that does not work, the dominant members of society will move further and further away from the problem. There have been few attempts to do something about the basic nature of the problem; that is, to create a more functional society in which more equitable opportunities exist. Actually, it seems that there is an attempt to avoid creating more equitable opportunities—at all costs.

Since this chapter deals with both the older and the young males, any application to the young male means that it has relevance for older males as well, since the young will eventually grow older. The point is that if these young males are being crippled at an early age, they will never become functional adults, leaving few eligible men for African American women. There are two problems here: one is that many young males, because of detrimental conditions, do not live to be adults; the other is that many of those who do survive are so crippled and disturbed that they are functionally useless as responsible citizens, companions, or caretakers of families.

References

Brunswick, A. (1988). Young Black males and substance use. In J. Gibbs (Ed.), Young Black and male in America: An endangered species (p. 166). Massachusetts: Auburn House Publishing Company.

Dembo, R. (1988). Delinquency among Black male youth. In J. Gibbs (Ed.), Young Black and male in America: An endangered species (p. 129). Massachusetts: Auburn House Publishing Company.

Gibbs, J. (1988). Young Black and male in America: An endangered species. Massachusetts: Auburn House Publishing Company.

Hatchett, D. (1986). … A conflict of reasons and remedies. Crisis, 93, 36.

Jones, K. (1986). The Black male in jeopardy. Crisis, 93, 19.

Kondracke, M. (1989, February). Two Black Americas. New Republic, 17-20.

Krisberg, B., Schwartz, I., Fishman, G., Eiskovits, Z., & Guttman, E. (1986). The incarceration of minority youth. Minneapolis: H. H. Humphrey Institute of Public Affairs, University of Minnesota.

Larson, T.E. (1988). Employment and unemployment of young Black males. In J. Gibbs (Ed.), Young Black and male in America: An endangered species (p. 97). Massachusetts: Auburn House Publishing Company.

Levy, W. (1986, August). Fathers who walk away. Ebony, 62.

Norment, L. (1986, August). Resolve tension between Black men and women. Ebony, 154.

Poussaint, A. (1986, August). Save the fathers. Ebony, 46.

Reed, R. (1988). Education and achievement of young Black males. In J. Gibbs (Ed.), Young Black and Male in America: An endangered species (p. 37) Massachusetts: Auburn House Publishing Company.

Riley, N. (1986). Footnotes of a culture at risk. Crisis, 93. 24.

Tolmach, J. (1985). There ain't nobody on my side. Journal of Child Clinical Psychology, 14, 214-219.

Wright, B. (1984). The psychopathic racial personality. Chicago: Third World Press.

PART IV

PRACTICAL APPROACHES TO WORKING WITH AFRICAN AMERICANS

Preliminary Comments

In this section of the book there are some practical approaches for working with African Americans. I discuss specific types of problems, and propose specific solutions. These are just a few of the many possible approaches that can be utilized when working with African Americans. As in working with any group or individual, the nature of the situation will dictate the best approach.

Chapter 9 puts forth an alternative conceptual model for diagnosing African Americans. It proposes that in order to understand the individual one must take into account the total socio-cultural context of the individual, including the roles that various institutions and organizations play within this environment.

Chapter 10 gives us some practical self-help strategies for coping with depression. It is assumed here that some clients won't be able to follow through with and continue in therapy. For these individuals a common sense list of do's and don'ts will go a long ways toward supporting the individual in a time of distress.

Chapter 11 proposes a conceptual model for counseling the violent offender in Black domestic relations. Domestic violence has reached alarming proportions in Black families. It is necessary that we work on finding ways to intervene effectively in these situations.

Chapter 12 deals with counseling at risk children. We must begin to work more effectively with our children. The children are our future, and we must save them. A three tiered approach is recommended in which the counselors, teachers, and parents seek to better serve the children

Chapter 9

An Alternative Conceptual Model for Diagnosing African Americans in Psychotherapy

Most psychotherapist when engaging in diagnoses tend to label the clients according to a specific diagnosis as seen in one of the various categories in the Diagnostic and Statistical Manual of Mental Disorders. If not this some therapists will be a little restrictive, and diagnose clients in more elaborate functional terms in regard to the nature of the problem: for example saying that a client has marital conflict because of not spending time with wife and children, and as a result both wife and children feel abandoned. The more elaborate functional diagnosis generally clarifies the functional nature of the specific problem: that is, giving a description of the dysfunction and saying how the disorder is manifested. In both these diagnoses the tendency is to label the problem in terms of pathology. In either case, the individual has caused or has contributed to a disease process that has manifested itself in the individual or the family. There is a disease or disorder that lies in the individual or family, and

This chapter was reprinted with permission from an article in the Quarterly, by the same title, number 129, page 2, spring 1993. It was also presented at the Annual Black Family Conference in Louisville, KY, March 13, 1993.

it is implied that this disease process must be treated by focusing on the problem. This is true of certain problem-centered therapies and especially in the medical model of psychotherapy.

In many cases therapists are unable to keep African Americans in psychotherapy, because they are not having their needs met. We point-the-finger at them when they become resistive and distrustful (Boyd-Franklin, 1984). Many times the problem is that therapists operate from premises and notions developed from false perceptions, and inaccurate labeling of the problem. It is suggested here that in most cases the problems that African Americans present are not individual problems, but are problems that relate to the socio-cultural context. Europeans might have more individual problems that require insight-oriented therapy, but most African American problems are derived from the socio-cultural context. Most of the problems of African Americans come from the environment in which they live: inadequate resources, lack of opportunities, oppression, discrimination, prejudice, and racism. Any attempt to see the problem of African Americans outside this socio-cultural context is in part a mislabeling of the problem (Nobles, 1980). Certainly, African Americans have problems that are individual, but in the final analysis, even these individual problems must be seen from within this socio-cultural context. Traditionally, in the African American community, the individual existed to serve the community, rather than the community existing to serve the individual (Jackson, 1983). The individual is a part of the community, is acted upon, is affected by and affects the community. The individual and the community are inseparable items. Problems arise for African Americans when they allow themselves to become separated from the ideas, values, and norms of the community.

What is needed is an alternative method of conceptualizing, viewing, and understanding the basic nature of the

African American client's problem. It is important to utilize a logical observational approach, one that will recognize the difference in the socio-cultural context and assist in reconnecting the disconnected individual or family to the identified system(s) (Sue & Zane, 1987). In the method proposed here, it is suggested that an alternative way of diagnosing the family or individual be implemented. This approach utilizes all aspects of the socio-cultural context: the world view systems; the environmental systems; the social, political, and economic systems; the cultural systems; the community systems; the helping systems; and the individual or family systems (see Figure 1). All of these systems are important when utilizing the socio-cultural context in making a diagnosis. The system in which the individual functions should be reviewed thoroughly, and a diagnosis made based on the position in the system where dysfunction has occurred. Diagnosis is not made based upon an individual problem, pathology or disorder, but is made based on a dysfunction in the larger socio-cultural context. Since the African American traditionally has been attached to and operating from a community base, it is important to utilize this larger socio-cultural context for diagnoses (Jenkins, 1985; Snowden, 1982).

The World View Systems

The largest possible and one of the most important systems we encounter in this model is the world view system. The world view system determine one's behavior, thought, feeling, attitude, the way the environment is viewed, and the way the person responds to relevant stimuli. The above are related to and dependent upon one's world view system. World view helps to determine culture and has a reciprocal relationship with culture. World view determines not only an individual's philosophical outlook; but, also the social, political, educational, economic, and religious outlook, as well as the physical design of the environment. It is necessary to take an in-depth look at this system, because of its potential impact on all other systems. There are two world view systems: Eastern and Western. Eastern and Western world views refer to the unique cultural way of life, characteristics, and dynamics expressed, as well as manifested by a people through their culture. Geographical, ethnic, and racial compositions are not the important determining factor of one's world view. For example Asians, Africans, and Indians are all a part of the Eastern world view system; but are not unified on any particular issues—only in world view (Burgest, 1989). A psychotherapist with a Western world view, especially if the Western world view therapist does not fully understand the theoretical orientation is in many ways systematically opposed to an Eastern theoretical orientation, and inadequate for diagnosing and treating Eastern individuals (Podair, 1967; Henle, 1965; Nobles, 1980; President's Commission on Mental Health, 1978). Principles from a Western world view system may have negative implications for a person from an Eastern world view. There is an assumption on the part of Western world view people that they are superior socially, intellectually and spiritually; this makes it difficult for therapist to establish rapport, a trusting relationship, or empathy with Eastern world view individuals. These feelings cause some problems in accurately perceiving the basic nature of the problems of an Eastern world view client. This is inherent because of the feelings of condescension, superiority, prejudice, and biases on the part of Western world view people (Burgest, 1989).

It is necessary to understand the idea of a world view system, and how Eastern world view individuals differ from Western world view individuals. The Eastern world view is characteristic of African Americans, and requires a different approach to diagnoses. Much of the difficulty psychotherapists have in making appropriate diagnoses and treatment plans for African Americans emanate from the fact that they evaluate clients from a theoretical orientation based on Eastern culture (Burgest, 1989; Sue, 1988). That is not to say that a therapist with a Western world view cannot provide treatment to an Eastern world view client. What is required for a therapist with either of these theoretical orientations to provide treatment to a client from the opposite theoretical orientation is that the therapist must be fully cognizant of the characteristics, dynamics, attitudes, beliefs, and perspectives of the client in the opposite orientation. The higher this level of awareness the more effective therapy will be. In addition, it will be necessary for the therapist to demonstrate a certain level of empathy, warmth, concern, and positive regard (Willis, 1990). Burgest (1989, p. 65) says: "European epistemological conception of their universe and their relationship to man, God, and nature can best be characterized as linear (Euro-linear) while the Eastern world view's conceptions of man, God, nature, and the universe can best be described as circular (Afro-circular)."

The Western world view. This view looks at matter, materials, forces, and entities in the universe as being in a hierarchy and separated into compartments, segments, divisions, dichotomies and conflicts. Things are separated into divisions and segments on a scale or continuum visualized on a horizontal line or vertical line. These forces that are divided and separated are at odds and in conflict with each other. There are conflicts between the individual/nature, God/devil, cause/effect, organic/inorganic, mind/body, and Black/white. The vertical or horizontal line is considered to be negative at one end and positive at the other. Usually a positive value is attached to the upper position on the continuum and a negative value attached to the lower position. This orientation has great implications for individuals and their relationship to other individuals. This way of viewing the world in dichotomies, opposites, and conflicts can be clearly seen in the negative and unfavorable definition of the concept of Blackness and the positive definition of the concept of whiteness (Burgest, 1989). This has caused white therapists to have a negative view of Blacks and their culture, causing it to be difficult for them to adequately diagnose and provide treatment for African Americans (Triandis & Brislin, 1984; Klineberg, 1985; Lefley, 1985). It is difficult for European psychotherapists to diagnose and provide treatment for African Americans when many Europeans have two basic conceptions of African Americans: that they are inferior, and their personality is abnormal. These conceptions have been promoted by the most respected social scientists, psychiatrists, religious leaders, and medical doctors throughout history (Thomas & Sillen, 1972; Freeman, Kaplan & Sadock, 1976; Bean, 1906; Bevis, 1921; Hall, 1904; Jarvis, 1844, 1852; Jensen, 1969; Morais, 1967; O'Mally, 1914; Stanton, 1960; Weatherly, 1910; White, 1903). Maultsby (1982) indicated that many Blacks are treated by European therapists, because at least 99% of psychotherapists are European; but even the Black therapists who constitute 1% are still being presented with a European world view. This is true because many Black therapists are educated in European institutions, books authored by whites constitute 98% of the required and recommended readings for both white and Black mental health students, and white mental health professionals do over 98% of America's mental health research. Chunn, Dunston & Ross-Sheriff (1983); Wyatt & Parham (1985) had a similar understanding of this situation.

The Eastern world view. The Eastern individual has a world view that is quite different from the Western individual. Eastern individuals believe that the essential unity of all things material and immaterial fosters the maintenance of harmony between God, the individual, nature, and the universe. Dichotomy, divisions, and separation between matter, materials, forces, and entities within the universe do not occur. Strife, odds, and conflict do not occur between God/devil, individual/nature, cause/effect, and mind/body. Harmony and unity are seen as existing between all forces and entities in the culture and society. Oneness, unity, togetherness, cohesion, and harmony can be described as a symbolic whole, and can be represented as a complete circle (Burgest, 1989). Burgest (1989) also used the following statements to conceptualize this symbol.

> The most ancient symbol known to man is the black circle or disc. This symbol represents the source of all life, knowledge, understanding and truth. The black circle is the womb, the great mother, the container of all that has been seen, is now and ever will be. The black circle symbolizes the undifferentiated state of spirit and matter, light and darkness, good and evil, male and female, and all other so-called opposites (p. 67).

Eastern individuals do not see themselves as separated from nature, nor significantly different from other individuals (Cedric, 1972).

> The Eastern/African philosophical statement that best captures its ideology is "I am because we are, therefore I am." The Implications of the statement "I am because we are, therefore I am" suggest unity, cohesion and oneness. It further suggests that the survival of an individual is intricately tied into the lives of other members of the society—those who have gone before and those who are yet to come. On the other hand, "I think therefore I am" places the individual at the height of the linear scale with "individuality" at the top, and all other forces, entities and matters at the bottom. This statement suggests that man can survive alone and without human contact or reinforcement from other humans, and we know that not to be true (Burgest, 1989, p. 69).

African Americans have been dominated by Western culture for generations. Whereas their fundamental orientation remains that of an Eastern world view tradition, there are distinct characteristics of each culture that differ to some degree—one from the other. In treating and diagnosing African Americans they must be seen from an Eastern world view perspective. If this does not take place, the therapist will fail to completely understand the individual. It is not difficult to understand that the Western social science theoretical base, with respect to treatment, is ineffective with African Americans (Maultsby, 1982: Burgest, 1989).

The Other Systems Within the Socio-Cultural Context.

The other systems in addition to the world view systems are also important. The other systems include the social, political, and economic systems; environmental systems; cultural systems; community systems; helping systems; and individual or family systems (see Figure 1). These systems are all a part of the socio-cultural context, and all systems are in part determined by the world view systems. The world view system is the largest system in the socio-cultural context, and it encapsulates all other systems within its boundaries. Individuals derive most of their values, ideas, concepts, attitudes, and beliefs from their socio-cultural context. When individuals act in a certain way, they are acting based on ideas and experiences conceptualized within their socio-cultural context. Our philosophy of life is based on ideas and principles found within our socio-cultural context. Better understanding of all the systems within our socio-cultural context is important to making an appropriate diagnosis, since the individual's functioning is based on these systems. An adequate diagnosis should be partially developed from an accurate assessment of the ideas, beliefs, and values found within the socio-cultural context. The way the educational, political, religious, and economic factors influence behavior are taken into account in this model. The political, economic, religious, and educational factors are utilized in the analysis as well as the social and psychological factors. All systems in the socio-cultural context are important; concentration should not be on any one particular system. Focusing on one aspect of the socio-cultural context is likely to lead to incomplete and inadequate diagnosis.

It is not a new idea to view one's socio-cultural context as important for understanding the conditions of the individual, but the context has not traditionally been assessed thoroughly and broadly in order to make an accurate diagnosis of the individual's problem. All the systems in the socio-cultural context, in many instances, have not been traditionally considered. In Figure 1 there is a diagram of the various

Figure 1. The socio-cultural context of an African-American individual or family.

systems that are a part of the socio-cultural context in which all African American individuals and families must function. It should be clear that in diagnosing an individual it is necessary to understand the socio-cultural context for the particular client that seeks treatment. For each client this socio-cultural context is different, if not in reality, at least in perception. Figure 1 displays a constantly expanding socio-cultural context as the circle progress outward, adding more systems to the total context. All the systems in the context are related and interdependent. The outermost circle has a relationship to all smaller circles within its boundaries. A therapist must understand the entire socio-cultural context before making an attempt to diagnose a client; and being familiar with this context will lead to more effective diagnosis. This model stresses system interconnectedness, culture, group identity and reciprocal benefit. The problems within these systems have multiple origins and require multiple approaches for solutions. It is important in these systems to have group focus and networks as crucial components in a diagnosis. The initial role of the therapist is one of understanding the problems that have developed in these systems, to help the client understand the difficulty, and ultimately to facilitate behaviors that will lead to better functioning involving multiple relationships within these systems.

Some important ideas, beliefs, and values within the socio-cultural context of African Americans. Listed below are several different therapists that have put forth ideas, beliefs, and values about systems within the African American socio-cultural context. These values and ideas are important because they define the socio-cultural context for African Americans. An understanding and awareness of values in the socio-cultural context will lead to more effective diagnoses. Most of these ideas have a similar vein of thought.

Jackson (1983) expressed the values in the African American socio-cultural context in the following manner:

1. Adaptive functioning is basic and very important to this context.

2. An emphasis is placed on "Wellness and normality" as opposed to psychopathology.

3. Strong kinship bonds with inherent feelings of cooperation and sharing are stressed.

4. Enhanced sensitivity to interpersonal issues are emphasized.

5. A strong religious orientation that provides structure, direction, a philosophy of the interrelatedness of all things, and a comprehensive way of interpreting the universe and life are characterized by this context.

6. Behaviors that derive from norms of the community are perceived as erosion of Black identity or cultural values. When this occurs re-socialization is needed.

7. The individual is not seen as having disordered development, and there is no reliance on individual recompensation, except as individual efforts are influenced by the group goals or extended self-identity.

Akbar (1976, 1977) felt the following were important to this socio-cultural context.

1. There is an absence of competitive attitudes; caring and concern are core behavior traits in this context.

2. In this context an affective orientation, respect for others, and drives are benevolent in nature—a desire to help others.

3. There is a holistic conceptual organization of the individual and the universe in this context.

Jackson (1976, 1977) felt similarly about the socio-cultural context of African Americans.

1. Social and political influences shape behavioral response in this context. Socialization experiences solidify group-centered behavior and parenting styles that cultivate

respect for age, cooperation, and role flexibility are all important.

2. In this context motivation is described as group-centered. This active process relies heavily on group consensual validation and facilitates reculturation.

Making a Diagnosis Utilizing the Socio-Cultural Context

Traditional methods of diagnosing start with talking to the client and making an assessment; this assessment will hopefully lead to a diagnosis that eventually will label the client as having a particular kind of problem. All diagnosis is for the ultimate purpose of assisting in the treatment process, by determining what kind of treatment would be most effective. Traditional methods of diagnosing have proven unsatisfactory for helping to accomplish the objectives of treatment with African Americans.

In the proposed alternative method of diagnosing, problems are not seen as individual problems, but emphasis is placed on the socio-cultural context. The individual is part of a family, a community, a culture; and should be seen, diagnosed, and treated from within this socio-cultural context. It should not be forgotten that African Americans are part of a culture, and that culture contains a circular-based logic which should be utilized to help the individual. An individual's ability to adapt, adjust, or function adequately in society may not be due to internal conflict. Problems in adapting and adjusting to Euro-American society may be a result of the conflicting and opposing values they must learn in order to function in this Western society (Burgest, 1989).

In simply labeling the individual, it is not felt that sufficient data has been collected to help make the individual better through treatment. According to traditional methods, by labeling the individual certain valuable insights can be gained that would help to specify particular methods of treatment. Another approach might yield a much higher success rate when diagnosing African American individuals or families.

The method proposed is to first make an assessment based upon the client's socio-cultural context. Once this assessment has been made, instead of labeling the client based on a disease-model, disorder or pathology, the therapist should first examine all the different systems involved in the client's problem. It is necessary to determine which systems are involved and how extensively. The diagnosis should be made based upon where it is felt that intervention is needed in the system(s).

Disconnection can occur within any of these systems. It is necessary to assess where the problems have occurred. Ultimately the knowledge gained from diagnoses can be used to help re-socialize the individual concerning dysfunctional problems in the particular system(s). The diagnosis should point out where, when and how problems have occurred. The diagnosis should illuminate understanding of the problems, and the issues surrounding the problems, as well as the functional nature of the problems. Treatment, the objective of diagnosis, will require re-socialization centered around the disconnections or problems in the system. The individual has been disconnected from one or more of the various systems and needs reconnecting. It is felt that the individual needs re-socialization because of having strayed away from norms of the community. The individual must be in syncronization with self, family, community, and culture. The degree that the individual strays away from values in these areas is the degree to which socialization is necessary (Jackson, 1983).

After determining the issue or nature of the problem, the therapist has the responsibility to assist the client to resolve the difficulties, recognizing the fact that African American individuals have an Eastern world view.

An example of the importance of the socio-cultural context in diagnosing and how it influences the person can be seen in religion. Religion is not a one-day affair but is a part of the individual's total being in the Eastern world view. Everything one does is intermixed with religion and cause and effect can be seen by the individual. It is difficult to work with an Eastern world view person without taking religion into account. Because of the experiences of African Americans they are more devoted to religion than most groups. In many cases God is the only one they feel they can depend on. Another example of the importance of the socio-cultural context can be seen in the Western world view: the concept of majority rule is placed at the top of the hierarchy in Western culture, while other individual concerns are secondary. In Eastern culture, the concept of consensus, unity, and oneness in decision making prevails and is circular in dimension (Burgest, 1989).

Case example (school phobia). An eight-year-old African American male came into a therapist office with his mother. The mother stated that her son needed counseling. The presenting problem was that her son was refusing to go to school. He cried and held on to her when it was time to board the school bus. When he did go to school, he asked his mother if she would be there when he got home.

On closer examination you find that the boy lives at home with his mother, grandfather, and four-year-old sister. His grandmother recently died, his step-brother died one month ago in a motorcycle accident, and he was very close to both these individuals. His father, to whom he was very close, left the family to take up residence with another female and her family. You find that these phobias began approximately two months ago. His mother suggested therapy, and the boy reluctantly agreed, but admitted that his fears were overwhelming.

We have already labeled the problem as a school phobia, therefore, it would seem that it is more important to place the situation in the proper socio-cultural context rather than giving it a label. It might also be labeled as an adjustment reaction or possibly grief for fear of further loss. The labels are appropriate because they help us become aware of what we are dealing with, but understanding the disconnectedness within the socio-cultural context is most important.

Looking at the scenario, we can say that this boy has become disconnected from his socio-cultural context in the following manner. He has school phobia because he is fearful that his mother will leave, and he will be alone with no one to care for him. In a child's mind when adult figures die or leave, it is in many cases seen by the child as blatant abandonment, and the fault of the child himself. The child was close and very connected to all of these individuals who either died or left on their own. When these individuals disappeared from the child's life, it was only natural for him to feel a sense of disconnection from his system. His family is not involved in very many community activities. The child's only connection with the community is the school and the church. He attends church with his mother and sister on a regular basis. He is from a working class family who usually tend to have fairly close ties to their family members. The family believes in unity and supports each other in times of trouble. There are no relationships with neighbors, friends, or community agencies, only strong immediate family. When a number of the immediate family members who were close to him disappeared, it was like his whole world had come apart. He then developed a phobia about his most important relationship—his mother. His thinking and his fear were that his mother would leave him just as the other members of his family had done. He was afraid that he would go to school one day, come home and find her missing—never to see her again. He was threatened by this possible loss as one that would be to overwhelming. He felt that it was necessary to keep his eyes on her so that this possibility would not happen.

For this eight-year-old boy it will not be necessary to examine other aspects of the socio-cultural context to develop an appropriate diagnosis. In some cases it will be necessary to examine other systems, and to examine them more closely.

It is clear that his boy needs reassurance that his mother will not leave or abandon him, that he will not suffer further loss of his family members—under ordinary circumstances. He needs to be more strongly connected to the remaining members of his family. If dad is available he should spend more time with his son. The boy should spend more time in the community developing friendships and involving himself in community activities. He should expand his support network to include more than only his immediate family.

Summary and Conclusion

It has been suggested here that in order to diagnose an individual adequately, it is first necessary to accurately perceive the individual within his/her socio-cultural context; secondly, to make an accurate assessment of the individual's situation within this context. The socio-cultural context is a complex set of systems that must be examined closely in order to determine the nature of the client's situation. Once this is done, an appropriate treatment plan can be developed, and an appropriate intervention strategy developed.

The most important system within the socio-cultural context is the world view. This system determines thought, action, and behavior in response to all other systems. Frequently, therapists, for one reason or the other, misinterpret this set of systems in the socio-cultural context. This causes therapists to treat individuals out of context.

In order to adequately diagnose and subsequently arrive at an adequate treatment strategy, it will be necessary to thoroughly understand the socio-cultural context of African American individuals. At this point it will be important to begin where the break has occurred in that particular system. Reconnection to the system where the break has occurred will be the action required. Without this reconnection, the client is seen as the problem, and is the focus of attention, while the actual problem does not receive adequate attention.

References

Akbar, N. (1976). The community of self. Chicago: Nation of Islam Office of Human Development.

Akbar, N. (1977). Natural psychology and human transformation. Chicago: World Community of Islam.

Bean, R.B. (1906). Some racial peculiarities of the Negro brain. American Journal of Anatomy, 5, 353-415.

Bevis, W.M. (1921). Psychological traits of the Southern Negro with observations as to some of his psychosis. American Journal of Psychiatry, 1, 69-78.

Boyd-Franklin, N. (1984). Issues in family therapy with Black families. Clinical Psychologist, 37, 54-58.

Burgest, D.R. (1989). Social work practice with minorities. New Jersey: The Scarecrow Press, Inc.

Cedric, C. (1972). Black studies on the study of Black people. In R. Jones (Ed.), Black psychology (pp. 3-17). New York: Harper & Row.

Chunn, J.C., Dunston, P.J., & Ross-Sheriff, F. (Ed.). (1983). Mental health and people of color: Curriculum development and change. Washington, D.C.: Howard University Press.

Freedman, A.M., Kaplan, H.I., & Shaddock, B.J. (1976). Modern synopsis of comprehensive textbook of psychiatry II (2nd ed.). Baltimore, MD: Williams & Wilkins Company.

Hall, G.S. (1904). Adolescence (Vol. 2). New York: Appleton.

Henle, P. (1965). Language, thought and action. Ann Arbor: University of Michigan Press.

Jackson, A.M. (1983). A theoretical model for the practice of psychotherapy. The Journal of Black Psychology, 10, 19-27.

Jackson, G. (1976). The African genesis of the Black perspective in helping. Professional Psychology, 7, 363-367.

Jackson, G. (1977). The emergence of a Black perspective in Counseling. Journal of Negro Education, 46, 230-253.

Jarvis, E. (1844). Insanity among the colored population of the free states. American Journal of Medical Sciences, 7, 71-83.

Jarvis, E. (1852). Insanity among the colored population of the free states. American Journal of Insanity, 8, 268-282.

Jenkins, A.H. (1985). Attending to self-activity in the Afro-American client. Psychotherapy, 22, 335-341.

Jensen, A.R. (1969). How much can we boost IQ and scholastic achievement? Harvard Educational Review, 39, 1-23.

Klineberg, O. (1985). The social psychology of cross-racial counseling. In P. Pedersen (Ed.), Handbook of cross-cultural counseling and therapy (pp. 29-36). Westport, CT: Greenwood.

Lefley, H.P. (1985). Mental health training across cultures. In P. Pedersen (Ed.), Handbook of cross-cultural counseling and therapy (pp. 173-179). Westport, CT: Greenwood.

Maultsby, M.C. (1982). Historical views of Blacks distrust of psychiatrist. In S. Turner & R. Jones (Eds.), Behavior modification in Black populations: Psychosocial issues and empirical findings (pp. 39-55). New York: Plenum Press.

Morais, H.M. (1967). The history of the Negro in Medicine. New York: Publishers Company, Inc.

Nobles, W. (1980). Extended self: Rethink the so-called Negro self-concept. In R.L.Jones (Ed.), Black psychology (pp. 99-105). New York: Harper & Row.

O'Mally, M. (1914). Psychosis in the colored race. Journal of Insanity, 71, 309-337.

Podiar, S. (1967, March) How bigotry builds through language. Negro Digest, pp. 38-43.

President's Commission on Mental Health. (1978). Report to the President. Washington, D.C.: U.S. Government Printing Office.

Snowden, L.R. (Ed.). (1982). Reaching the undeserved: Mental health needs of neglected populations. Beverly Hills, CA: Sage.

Stanton, W. (1960). The leopard's spots: Scientific attitudes toward race in America 1815-1859. Chicago: University of Chicago Press.

Sue, S., & Zane, N. (1987). The role of culture and cultural techniques in psychotherapy: A critique and reformulation. American Psychologist, 42, 37-45.

Sue, S. (1988). Psychotherapy services for ethnic minorities: Two decades of research findings. American Psychologist, 43, 301-308.

Thomas, A., & Sillen, S. (1972). Racism and psychiatry. New Jersey: The Citadel Press.

Trandis, H.C., & Brislin, R.W. (1984). Cross-Cultural psychology. American Psychologist, 39, 1006-1016.

Weatherly, U.G. (1910). Race and marriage. American Journal of Sociology, 15, 433-454.

White, W.A. (1903). The geographic distribution of insanity in the United States. Journal of Nervous and Mental Diseases, 30, 257-279.

Willis, J.T. (1990) Implications for effective psychotherapy with African-American families and Individuals. Matteson, Illinois: Genesis Publications.

Wyatt, G.E., & Parham, W.D. (1985). The inclusion of culturally sensitive course materials in graduate schools and training programs. Psychotherapy, 22, 461-468.

Chapter 10

Self-Help Strategies for African Americans in Coping with Depression

---

Introduction

Depression is a common phenomenon, both in the African American community as well as in many other communities. Racism as a factor certainly contributes to this depression in the African American community. Much of this depression goes untreated as long as it does not reach the clinically depressed stage. In this chapter the focus is on self-help strategies that are useful for helping to alleviate depression when it has its basis in racism.

It is considered here that most often racism contributes to a milder form of depression, and mild depression is the focus.

Though, racism as a cause of clinical depression should not necessarily be ruled out. When clinical depression

---

This chapter was presented to the Second Midwest Regional Conference on Black Families and Children, Overland Park, Kansas, June 13, 1994. It was also published, with slight modifications, in the Black Caucus, Number 3, fall 1994.

is the outcome of racism, it should be treated with combinations of Psychotherapy and pharmacotherapy—regardless of the cause. It should also be understood that milder forms of depression, if left untreated, may eventually turn into clinical depression.

Operational definition of depression. Again, it should be clear from the outset that in this chapter we are only considering the milder forms of depression. Depression generally has a very clear, precise and understood meaning; but, it is useful to here give an operational definition of depression. Depression can generally be defined as anger turned inward, resulting in specific symptoms. Hughley (1992) a recent theoretician and long-time practitioner in the field of psychotherapy, who developed an approach to counseling called Copology, gives a definition that adds new dimensions to the concept of depression. He says that, "Depression is internalized anger and fear." He believes that there are three basic emotions: love, anger, and fear. Hughley feels that anger and fear are two different basic emotions. Anger has a function that is different from the function of fear: the function of anger is action, designed to prevent loss or provide correction for losses; the function of fear is attention to loss—potential or actual loss. The intensity of the struggle to resist carrying out the function of the emotions (anger and fear) consumes much of the person's energy. This reduces the person's capacity to be attentive to the outside world, leading to a short attention span, fatigue, reduced activities, lack or increase of motivation to eat, and problems with self care. The primary cause of this depression is that there is resistance of the individual to carry out the functions of fear and anger. The pain of fear and anger builds because the person fails to carry out the functions of these emotions.

Milder forms of sadness, withdrawal, sleep disturbances and anxiety, loss of appetite, reduced sexual drive, and physical energy can be considered mild depression.

When these symptoms persist or get worse the person is headed for a clinical depression, and should seek psychotherapy, pharmacotherapy or combinations of these (Papolos & Papolos, 1987). "When depressed, a person often dwells on exaggerated memories of losses or failures, or focuses on the morbid and negative aspects of life to the exclusion of all other things. A person may experience persistent feelings of sadness and emptiness, become tearful for no apparent reason or become irritable and hostile. The depressed person may be slowed down, lack energy and have fewer ideas" (1987, P. 4).

Why necessary to consider self-help. When African Americans grow-up believing that the only reason they don't succeed is their own inadequacies, one of the outcomes is to internalize their failure, which may eventually lead to depression. We must not blame the victim, and see ourselves as responsible for our own situation—in many cases, nor the situation of society. Many in the current generation have been isolated enough to begin to believe this. It is necessary to overcome these issues to realize that there are some external factors in these individual scenarios. These individuals must realize that there are limits placed upon them by society; that some of these situations they can't control. Part of the self-help strategies will involve learning what they can and cannot control, as well as learning not to feel demoralized as a result of their difficulties.

In a psychiatric epidemiology survey in St. Louis, African Americans sought care less frequently than European Americans for depression, mainly because of fear of treatment and fear of being hospitalized. The system is more intimidating to African Americans than it is to whites. Many African Americans consider depression to be a normal outcome of everyday problems, stresses, and strains; not to be taken as a serious psychiatric illness. Only when a complete breakdown in relationships with family, friends, and children occurs, are many African Americans likely to seek help. Many of them see depression as physical rather than an emotional illness. Since we know that an informal network of friends, relatives, extended family, church, and alternative healers or folk practitioners play important roles in African American society, it makes sense to develop and consider self-help strategies that might aid African Americans in dealing with depression related to racism (Felton, Robins, & Sussman, 1987).

Because many African American clients cannot afford long-term counseling, have other priorities, or do not have the motivation to continue with an involved psychotherapeutic process, it is necessary to give the clients some practical self-help strategies during the limited time the clients make themselves available. Many clients either do not return after one session or continue only for a limited number of sessions. In most cases the problem for which the client initially sought help continues to be an issue. The objective should be to help the client as much as possible to deal with the depressed condition. In view of this fact, the objective is to help the therapist to be able to give the client some self-help strategies that are useful without continued dependence on the therapist, or at least some strategies to use while not in the presence of the therapist.

Historical Background/Literature Review

At any given time about 3% of men and 6% of women are clinically depressed. Depression has been slowly rising in incidence in people born since the 1940s. Baby boomers are three to six times more likely to report a depression than those born at the turn of the century. Some causes of this increase are considered to be higher expectations from life and diminished family stability (Wartik, 1992a). Seligman (1992) reported that 11,500,000 are afflicted with clinical depression. Each year this disease drains $27,000,000,000 from our national economy because of loss of productivity. Americans lose approximately 177,000,000 days from work per year due to this disorder. Seventy percent of all cases of suicide are influenced by this disorder. Approximately 20 million Americans at some point in their lives will suffer from this illness (Goode, 1990). Others estimate that between eight and fifteen million suffer from this illness at any given time. It is not known how many people suffer from mild depression, because most people never get treated for mild depression, it should be obvious that due to this fact it is difficult to get accurate statistics. The problem, again, in many cases of mild depression, if not treated, may eventually turn into clinical depression. This point cannot be excessively emphasized.

In reviewing the literature, it was found that very little has been written about depression on African Americans as a separate category of individuals. It is even more difficult to find information on how racism is related to depression in African Americans. There has been very little investigation of treatments for different racial groups (Fellin, 1989). Most of the ideas here come from the experiences of the author while in the process of doing psychotherapy. The present technology in mental health does not reveal all causes of depression, but clearly racism is one contributory cause of depression. Racism certainly causes a deflation of one's self-esteem to the extent that there is a lowered self-evaluation. It has been proven that lowered self-esteem contributes to depression. The problems that African Americans experience leads to lack of self-esteem, and lack of self-esteem leads to depression (Beck, 1967; Adler, Andrews, Bridge, Brown & Harris, 1986; Brown & Harris 1978)). Papolos and Papolos (1987) stated that, "Negative thoughts or perceptions about oneself can erode self-esteem, resulting in an unrealistic sense of worthlessness and the feelings of being a burden to others" (p. 4). Hammen (1991); Angell, Monroe, Simmons, and Thase (1993); Kirk (1986) recognized that stress causes many physical and psychological maladies. Negative life events cause stress, and stress can lead to depression. "Stress is significantly related to the degree and amount of power that one perceives he or she has within the societal context" (Kirk, 1986, p. 4). African Americans have very little, real or perceived power, within the American society. This can result in a great deal of stress. Stress can also be considered a contributory factor to depression in African Americans. Kwon and Whisman (1993) also noted that stress in one's environment can lead to depression. Because of the position that African Americans occupy in the U.S. society, a certain amount of depression is bound to occur. It is difficult to live in a supposedly equalitarian society and be curtailed day after day, without developing some physical and psychological symptoms. "Living under such circumstances is very stressful. It can cause a person to question his or her worth as a human being and creates a negative self-concept" (Kirk, 1986, p. 5). It can also lead to internal rage, which may contribute to depression (1986). Kessler and Neighbors (1986) analyzed eight epidemiology surveys and found that a combination of the stress of racial discrimination, compounded by poverty, leads to higher levels of depressive symptoms among African Americans. Eaton and Kessler (1981) found that African Americans are at a much greater risk for depression, due to discrimination and poverty. They found that unemployment was also related to depressive symptoms. Dressler (1986) also studied unemployment and depressive symptoms in a southern African American community and found that unemployment is related to higher rates of depressive symptoms in the African American community. Gray and Jones (1987), Barbee (1992) suggest that African American women are more likely than white women to have depressive disorders. The cause of distress is because of their double-bind position—being African American and female.

To be African American and conscious is to be in a perpetual state of anger and rage. African Americans exist in a state of psychic toll and uninterrupted anger; this makes it difficult for them to cope with life. Most of this anger is directed inward, because it is one of the few acceptable vents or releases for this anger. Clearly anger directed inward can cause depression (Alexander & French, 1948; Biaggio & Godwin, 1987; Grainger, 1990; Moore & Paolillo, 1984; White, 1977). It should not be necessary to establish that racism exist in America, but only necessary to say that this constant pressure devaluates the self-esteem of African Americans. Anger, stress, and devaluated self-esteem certainly leaves individuals vulnerable to depression (Ingham, Kreitman, Miller, & Sashidharan, 1989; Adler, Andrews et al., 1986; Andrews & Brown, 1993). A number of other authors found that the stress of daily living in addition to low self-esteem left people especially vulnerable to depression (Andrews, Bifulco, Brown & Veiel, 1990; Andrews, Bifulco & Brown, 1990; Bolger, De Longis, Kessler, & Schilling, 1989; Eckenrode, 1984; Ingham, Kreitman, Miller, & Sashidharan, 1989).

Self-Help Strategies

There are a number of ways to treat depression: psychotherapy, pharmacotherapy, combinations of these two, psychosocial, physical or self-help methods. The assumption here is that a therapist will have an opportunity to see the client for at least one to several sessions, and be able to impart these strategies to the client. Obviously, it won't be extremely productive to give self-help strategies on treating depression to psychotherapist, without these ideas being somehow transmitted to the clients. It is assumed that these self-help methods will be given to the client by the therapist when economic or other considerations prevent more than minimal therapy sessions from taking place. By following some of these self-help strategies, individuals can spend less time despairing, being impaired and ill, and more time being fulfilled, productive, and healthy. Biological, genetic, and psychological factors contribute to this illness. There are many suggested causes for depression. Only one environmental cause is considered here. When clients are clinically depressed they should never try to use self-help strategies, but get adequate professional help.

African Americans are exposed to a society that condemns them as useless and non-functional. As a group they internalize these ideas generated by the larger society. In addition, society reinforces these ideas on a daily basis, to the extent that they begin to believe that they are the problem. Because African Americans have been defined negatively, it becomes easy for their character to be deflated. Lack of unity as a group leads them to further internalize and individualize the problem. Each individual then tends to believe that there is something internal that causes them to be the way they are. They then internalize their frustration which leads to depression.

The "pathological triangle." African Americans exist in what can be described as a "pathological triangle." They are constantly defined by the society in negative terms. As a whole most African Americans have been unable to achieve satisfactorily in most aspects of society. They exist in a society that is racist; this leads them to experience negativity in the work place, and consequently a negative family situation (see Figure 1). There is no safe haven: they get degraded at home, on the job, and in the general society. This "pathological triangle" leads to depression in the African American. If an individual does not have a place to relax and be comfortable, the resulting anxiety is translated to all those who meet the individual. The most susceptible individual is the one who has no means of venting the subsequent frustration, and thus is more likely to internalize it. In many situations, there are only a few known desirable places for the individual to relax and release tension except drugs, bars, and through other types of negativity. The individual will use these sources until they no longer work. At this point the individual will begin to internalize the frustration… .Because we are constantly demeaned and degraded by the larger society, we allow ourselves to be easily frustrated by the slightest implication that these things are true. We let other people upset us who know they can push our buttons so very easily, leading to greater anger and frustration. Because we have been defined in such negative terms, it becomes easy for our character to be deflated.

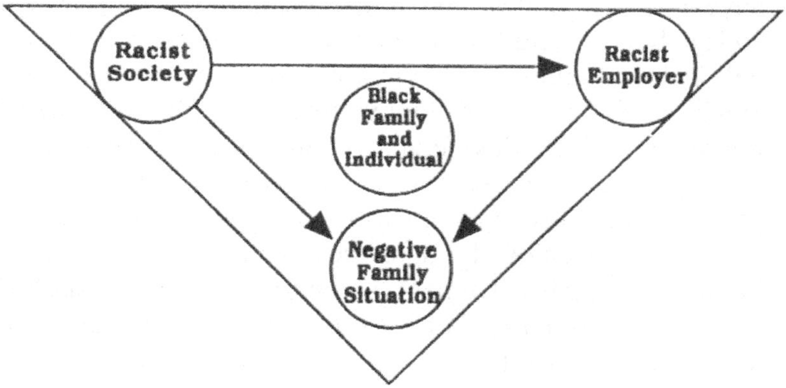

Figure 1. The "pathological triangle" of the African-American.

Taking control of our lives. We must realize that we cannot be responsible for the actions of others. One can only control their own thoughts and actions. We should not respond emotionally, but show others the error of their ways. We must remove ourselves from being responsible for what happens in the society—especially things out of our control. We do not have to constantly be on the defensive, or always justifying our existence. African Americans need to develop a sense of self, and an understanding of racism.

It is necessary to impart the following ideas to the client for his or her own use. One should have a proper diet, get plenty of exercise, and relax whenever possible. This reduces anxiety and tension. Exercise has been shown to fight depression. It helps rid you of tension so that you can sleep better, and research suggests it may positively affect certain brain chemicals that control mood (Wartik, 1992a). A basic diet of nutrient/rich foods—cottage cheese, carrots, tuna, baked potatoes, or even honey may be helpful. Some foods contain a mood booster called serotonin (1992a). Look for solutions, don't isolate yourself, develop a close family unit, have a social outlet, and a friendship network (Dressler, 1985). It is generally accepted that a good social network will help to relieve the symptoms of depression (Hickey, 1991; Veiel, 1993). Surround yourself with optimistic people (Grainger, 1990). Make human contact; having someone express concern can be a good treatment. Join with other people and get involved in various activities. Get involved in activities you enjoy; be sure these activities require maximum effort and involvement. Learn to master a new skill. Do something in order to feel a sense of accomplishment. Don't think about it, just do it. Go out and have a delicious dinner. Demonstrate to yourself that you are not worthless. Don't focus on yourself or ruminate, try to get out of yourself, and to focus on other aspects of your environment (Grainger, 1990; Neale, Rachmiel, Saltzberg, Stone, & Wood, 1990). Remember that some things you have power over and some you don't, but you can choose how to respond to something. You should identify the problem and ask; can I take full control of it, or partial control, or must I just learn to let go? (Wartik, 1992). Slow down and relax mentally, spiritually, and emotionally. Do not offer your emotions for attack. Be content with who you are, what you are, and what you are able to accomplish. One must learn to strive for the best, but to always be contented with who and what one is. Respect yourself and all others who do not indicate that they are undeserving of this respect. Take charge of your life and the lives of the children that you continue to be responsible for. Be determined to keep your dreams and aspirations alive. Be supportive to family and friends—especially. Practice love, understanding and patients in all of your daily activities. Believe in yourself and your capabilities. We should always strive to love, respect, understand self, and have determination and perseverance. Set short-term goals that are possible to achieve (Cantanzaro, 1991). One should express concern but not criticism to the depressed individual. The depressed must be carefully guided toward help. Let them know you care.

The client must understand the following things about depression. Depression is just like a bully, it will kick you around if you let it; you have to force yourself to take charge. You must force yourself to get up and begin to engage in activities of the day. You must do something constructive. Depression feeds on inertia, and action is its natural enemy. The less you do the less you want to do, to fight inertia, you have to simply devise a plan of action and execute it. Break complicated activities into simple and smaller task; they will seem much more manageable. You can't wait until you feel better, you may never feel better if you don't take some action. Take a small step to get started, even if you are not in the mood. Before you do anything, try smiling—instead of frowning, or sitting up straight—instead of slumping over, take a few deep breathes, and hold your head high. Sitting slumped forward or looking downward, and sighing gloomily can bring on a feeling of depression. Don't drag your feet, walk lively, don't slouch; our behavior can shape our emotions. An occasional cup of coffee or a soft drink can act as an antidepressant (Grainger, 1990).

Our home or apartment should be kept bright, cheerful, and neat; as opposed to dull, gloomy, and desolate. When you can, spend time in bright sunlight instead of in a gloomy situation (Grainger, 1990). This contributes to one's feeling of well-being and comfort. It has a lot to do with the way one feels about themselves. Reading cheerful and enjoyable books will get some people in the right mood. Try capturing your feelings and thoughts toward your problems on paper. Involve yourself in meaningful work (Lashmar, 1994). Learn to identify your depressed feelings and work on them before they get the best of you (Grainger, 1990). Kirk (1986) suggests that:

> Blacks can alleviate these conditions by being aware of the social, economic, and political restraints within which they exist. This should lead to more realistic expectations regarding their degree of assimilation into the White American society at any given time. It should also increase their degree of Black consciousness and enhance their self-esteem. An aspect of good mental health is an awareness both of what is not possible and what is possible. This is not to suggest that people should lower their drives or expectations, but that they should look at a given situation more realistically in terms of their own ability and in terms of the external factors that may add to or interfere with this ability to achieve goals (p. 8).

Learn to express your Anger. You must learn to express your anger and fear, don't suppress it. Don't destroy property or attack someone, but acknowledge the anger and fearful feelings; find out why you are angry and express the anger, but in a way that doesn't hurt yourself or others. Expressing such anger in a socially acceptable way may eradicate it. Admit the anger and fear and find useful ways to express it (Grainger, 1990). Suppressing emotions can result in numerous physical and psychological complications—one is depression. Emotions can start our thinking: if we think angrily, we may become angry. If we stop and think about the problem, and look for a solution instead, this anger and fear may find the proper channel for expression. We should express anger and fear by directing it outward (Anderson & Clay, 1993; Riley, Treiber, & Woods 1989). Though not generally considered acceptable for a man, crying can bring relief from the emotions of fear and anger. By crying one carries out the function of fear and anger. This crying brings attention to the potential loss and can prevent further loss by engaging one to act to prevent further loss. Crying is only one example of carrying out the function of one's emotions. Hughley (1992) feels that it is necessary to carry out these functions before relieving the pain of fear and anger. When this fear and anger build to a high point of intensity, it can cause depression or some other physical or psychological problem.

The person should then develop their conscious level to the fullest extent possible. Understanding one's history will help to develop a higher level of consciousness. Provide self with positive, empowering thoughts, and always focus on the positive. By doing these things a person can lead a more productive life without crippling depressive symptoms related to a negative society.

Implications for Service Delivery, Education, and Research

This chapter clearly demonstrates that racism can contribute to depression in African Americans; but, it is necessary to do more research in this area. More research would be able to clarify what are the specific factors and variables involved in this process. Service delivery could also be greatly enhanced by facilitating the person's ability to use self-help strategies. Appropriate service delivery could prevent the onset of more severe forms of clinical depression, as a result of lack of intervention. If racism is definitely a cause of a milder form of depression, and self-help strategies are found effective in treating this depression, educational programs should be set up to provide more self-help strategies for depression as a general part of the educational curriculum of African Americans. This would cause African Americans to be less susceptible to these milder forms of depression related to racism.

Conclusion

We are losing the war on many fronts in fighting racism. Racism has many ugly heads. The stress from racism can cause and exacerbate many different types of physical illnesses, as well as many psychological illnesses. We have tried to establish that racism is a contributory cause to depression in African Americans. Racism is not losing ground in this or any other country. It will be important, therefore, to learn to fight it or be crippled by it. We have already lost too many casualties; we can not afford to lose many more. We must learn to cope with depression caused by racism, or continue to be overwhelmed by this condition, which causes many individuals to be virtually non-functional.

References

Adler, Z., Andrews, B., Bridge, L., Brown, G.W., & Harris, T.O. (1986). Social support, self-esteem, and depression. Psychological Medicine, 16, 813-831.

Alexander, F.G., & French, T.M. (1948). Studies in psychosomatic medicine: An approach to the cause and treatment of vegetative disturbances. New York: Ronald.

Anderson, W.P., & Clay, D.L. (1993). Relationship between anger expression and stress in predicting depression. Journal of Counseling and Development, 72, 91-94.

Andrews, B., & Brown, G.W. (1993). Self-esteem and vulnerability to depression: The current validity of interviews and questionnaire measures. Journal of Abnormal Psychology, 102, 565-572.

Andrews, B., Bifulco, A., & Brown, G.W. (1990). Self-esteem and depression: Aetiological issue. Social Psychological and Psychiatric Epidemiology, 2, 235-243.

Andrews, B., Bifulco, A., Brown, G.W., & Veiel, H. (1990). Self esteem and depression: Measurement issues and prediction of onset. Social psychiatry and Psychiatric Epidemiology, 25, 200-209.

Angell, K.L., Monroe, S.M., Simmons, S.D., & Thase, M.E. (1993). Cognition and life stress in depression: Cognitive factors and the definition, rating, and generation of negative life events. Journal of Abnormal Psychology, 102, 584-591.

Barbee, E.L. (1992). African-American women and depression: A review and critique of the literature. Archives of Psychiatric Nursing, 6, 257-265.

Beck, A.T. (1967). Depression: Clinical, experimental and theoretical aspects. London: Staples.

Biaggio, M.K., & Godwin, W.H. (1987). Relation of depression to anger and hostility constructs. Psychological Reports, 61, 87-90.

Bolger, N., De Longis, A., Kessler, R.C., & Schilling, E.A. (1989). Effects of daily stress on negative mood. Journal of Personality and Social Psychology, 75, 808-818.

Brown, G.W., & Harris, T.O. (1978). Social origins of depression: A study of psychiatric disorder in women. London: Tavistock.

Catanzaro, S. J. (1991). Adjustment, depression, and minimal goal setting: The moderating effect of performance feedback. Journal of Personality, 59, 243-261.

Dressler, W.W. (1985). Extended family relationship, social support, and mental health in a southern Black community. Journal of Health and Social Behavior, 26, 39-48.

Dressler, W.W. (1986). Unemployment and depressive symptoms in a southern Black community. Journal of Nervous and Mental Disease, 174, 639-645.

Eaton, W.W., & Kessler, L.C. (1981). Rates of symptoms of depression in a national sample. American Journal of Epidemiology, 114, 528-538.

Eckenrode, J. (1984). Impact of chronic and acute stressors on daily reports of mood. Journal of Personality and Social Psychology, 46, 907-918.

Fellin, P. (1989). Perspectives on depression among Black Americans. Health and Social Work, 14, 245-252.

Felton, E., Robins, L.N., & Sussman, L.K. (1987). Treatment-seeking for depression by Black and white Americans. Social Science & Medicine, 24, 187-196.

Goode, E.E. (1990, March 5). Beating depression. U.S. News & World Report, pp. 48-56.

Grainger, R.D. (1990). Depression. Journal of Nursing, 90, 13-14.

Gray, B.A., & Jones, B.E. (1987). Psychotherapy and Black women: A survey. Journal of the national Medical Association, 79, 177-181.

Hammen, C. (1991). Generations of stress in the course of unipolar depression. Journal of Abnormal Psychology, 100, 555-561.

Hickey, M.C. (1991, January). Keeping up when you're feeling down. Parent's Magazine, pp. 53-60.

Hughley, G. (1992). Copology: The fifth force. Unpublished manuscript.

Ingham, J.G., Kreitman, N.B., Miller, P. McC., & Sashidharan, S.P. (1989). Self-esteem, life stress and psychiatric disorder. Journal of Affective Disorders, 17, 65-75.

Kessler, R., & Neighbors, H. (1986). A new perspective on the relationship among race, social class and psychological distress. Journal of Health and Social Behavior, 27, 107-115.

Kirk, A.R. (1986). Destructive behaviors among members of the Black community with a special focus on males: Causes and methods of intervention. Journal of Multicultural Counseling and Development, 14, 3-9.

Kwon, P., & Whisman, M.A. (1993). Life stress and dysphoria: The role of self-esteem and hopelessness. Journal of Personality and Social Psychology, 65, 1054-1059.

Lashmar, P. (1994). No hope no despair. New Statesman and Society, 7, 18-19.

Moore, T.W., & Paolillo, J.G. (1984). Depression: Influence of hopelessness, locus of control, hostility and length of treatment. Psychological Reports, 54, 875-881.

Neale, J.M., Rachmiel, T.B., Saltzberg, J.A., Stone, A.A. & Wood, J.V. (1990). Self-focused attention, coping response, and distressed mood in everyday life. Journal of Personality and Social Psychology, 58, 1027-1036.

Papolos, D.F., & Papolos, J. (1987). Overcoming depression. New York: Harper & Row, Publishers.

Riley, N.T., Treiber, F.A., & Woods, M.G. (1989). Anger and hostility in depression. Journal of Nervous and Mental Disease, 177, 668-674.

Seligman, M.E.P. (1992, January-February). Wednesday's children. Psychology Today, p. 61.

Veiel, H.O.F. (1993). Detrimental effects of kin support networks on the course of depression. Journal of abnormal Psychology, 102, 419-429.

Wartik, N. (1992, December). Blue moods. Working woman, pp. 81-94.

Wartik, N. (1992a, December). Bouncing back. Working Woman, pp. 84-94.

White, R.B. (1977). Current psychoanalytic concepts of depression. In W. Fann, I. Karacan, A. Pokorny, & R. Williams (Eds.), Phenomenology and treatment of depression (pp. 127-141). New York: Spectrum.

Chapter 11

A Conceptual Model for Counseling the Violent Offender in Black Domestic Relations

Introduction

Violence in the family dates back to the time of Cain and Abel, though the idea of family violence is relatively new. The earliest identified, and most recognized form of family violence, was physical abuse against children. Society now recognizes that there are many forms of violence occurring in the family. This chapter will specifically relate to counseling with the violent offender in Black domestic relations. The end product will be a working model for counseling with the Black violent offender. It will be necessary to arrive at this model through a process of giving consideration to the socio-historical and present context of the Black family. This process involves considering why the Family is the way it is. A large proportion of the time is spent on the process of developing the model. It should be kept in mind that the process of arriving at the conceptualization is just as

This chapter was presented to the annual Black family Summit, North Charleston, South Carolina, February 25, 1994; and, at the National Black Family Conference, Louisville, Kentucky, March 9, 1995. It was also published in the Family Therapy Journal, 21, 139-148, 1994.

important as the end product. By following and understanding the process of conceptualization, one can get the full benefit of how the model was developed, and how it can be utilized.

Incidence of Black family violence. National statistics on family violence are difficult to interpret and compare, because there is very little consistency in how information is collected. Statistics are unreliable because much of this violence goes unreported. Definitions of what constitutes family violence may vary from state to state, as do methods of counting the violent activity. It is virtually impossible to know what occurs in the privacy of the home. This being the case, it is very difficult to get all of these categories broken down and analyzed on a national level, and accurate statistics produced. Most of the statistics presently being produced are derived from isolated surveys from a particular state. It is even more difficult to get statistics for some of the categories of Black family violence (Landes, Siegel & Foster, 1993). Violent family activities occur in several different areas of family violence, that can then be further subdivided, and it is fairly difficult to get adequate statistics on all of these areas: Child abuse and neglect (physical, mental), spouse abuse (physical, mental), parent abuse (physical, mental), elder abuse (physical, mental), homicide, and other family member abuse are all possibilities. Some of the categories of family violence goes unrecognized as statistical categories. In most cases the statistics given are for the society in general. It has been generally considered that violence in the family was perpetuated by the male against other family members. This is not necessarily the case, though there is a dearth of statistics on some of the other categories. Violence includes all categories of abuse, whether it be actual hitting or not—violence can be psychological. Since these activities are difficult for the authorities of government to follow statistically, a very limited idea about the extent of this violence exists. Since violence among the poor and Blacks specifically, either equal or exceed that for the general population, the statistics given are a good indicator of how much violence actually occurs in the Black family. It is known that Blacks have a disproportionate amount of family violence when compared to other groups. Because the statistics available can be rather misleading, an attempt has been made to minimize the amount of statistics given, to avoid confusion.

The frequency of husbands' abuses of their spouses is estimated at 3-4,000,000 incidents a year, resulting in 1,000,000 injuries, while many incidents go unreported. Every second a woman is battered in her home; 25-45% has been beaten during the pregnancy, and 40% have been raped during the pregnancy. Injuries sustained from battering during pregnancy often result in babies with low birth weight, one of the biggest risks to an infant's well being, normal growth, and future development. Family violence is also associated with miscarriages and premature labor, and is the most frequent reason women visit emergency rooms. Physical and emotional abuse accounts for 25% of all female suicide attempts, and more than 4,000 homicides per year. Thus, this is an interpersonal and social problem of enormous magnitude (Holtz & Furniss, 1991). An estimated 2.4 million children are alleged victims of child abuse and neglect per year. Every year some 1,000 of these children die from their injuries. In 1990 there were 1.5 million confirmed cases of child abuse and neglect. Approximately three children die each day from abuse or neglect. Since 1980, reports of child abuse and neglect have quadrupled. This abuse and neglect occur at tremendous economic and psychological cost to its victims. As mentioned previously, few sources give separate statistics for the Black family. Jones (1993) noted that approximately 500,000 cases of Black child abuse and neglect are reported yearly. Child abuse and neglect is up 40% in Blacks since 1985. The child abuse and neglect rate for Blacks in 1985 was 15.7 per 100; for whites it was 10.3 per 100, a considerably higher rate for Blacks. From

1975 to 1985 the rate for whites decreased, but remained the same for Blacks (Landes, Siegel & Foster, 1993).

History. The experience of slavery and subsequent treatment has affected Blacks in such a way as to influence the dynamics within the family structure. This, in effect, causes the Black family to behave differently from other groups in regard to its members, and to manifest its pathology in different ways. The Black family has had many disruptions to its normal ability to function, but the experience of a history of many invasions, the Middle-Passage, and slavery caused the situation of the family to be constituted differently than most groups. The role of the Black male and female was perverted, in that they were denied the right to be parents and protectors. As a result, the female by default assumed the major responsibilities of the household. This confusion in roles was passed on from one generation to another; many Black males still have been unable to assume responsibility for their role as husband and father. The female, in many cases, still bears the responsibility for nurturing the family (Green, 1975). The female experienced much frustration out of having to take responsibility for these roles. The female lost some respect for the male in slavery that has not been regained—even today. The situation is compounded because of present environmental constraints placed on the male and female.

> Blacks were raped of their history and culture; were told that they were worthless; were told they had no legal rights; were lynched; were forced to hate other blacks; were told they should not or could not own property; were told that they were lazy and uneducable; and were discriminated against in the educational system, the economic system, the psychological system, the medical system, the political system, and the social system. It is against this background of deceit, oppression, misuse, exploitation, enslavement, court

> battles, sit-ins... marches on Washington... participation in 'black is beautiful' movements; and of watching white public officials in the nation's capital cut or eliminate federal and local programs that are designed to help black Americans, that we, blacks and whites, have arrived where they are in the United States today (Smith, 1978, p. 88).

These types of issues still plague the family, and cause the need for it to deal with additional pathologies when compared with other groups. The female has taken the stance that she deserves all the amenities that society has to offer; but the male has been unable to provide these amenities. It has become difficult for the male and female to live up to one another's standards, creating a very real schism in the family structure. This puts the male and female on two different levels and adds additional confusion and conflict to black family relationships in present-day America.

> With slavery, black families were separated ergo-bonding and the extended family network was discouraged. In post-slavery society, the psychological scars that remained were further intensified by continuing personal and institutional racist practices that devalue personal worth and family pride. An example of this phenomenon is the black male's relegation to positions of psychological and socioeconomic impotence in relation to his family. It must be remembered, furthermore, that in addition to the stresses of racism, black families must face problems common to all American families (Lyles & Carter, 1982, p. 1120).

Discrimination, economic isolation, couple with a lack of appreciation of their culture, and denigration of their ethnic status, have had a devastating impact on the Black family. Although large numbers of families have recently begun to show signs of stress from factors related to economic and geographic changes, regardless of race (McAdoo, 1977); Black families have the additional burden of their ethnic group being evaluated negatively, and, "While coping with the developmental crisis faced by all families, continuing pressures of institutional and personal racism bear heavily on them" (1977, p. 77). In addition, the media have been purveyors of false stereotypes of the Black family.

Present socio-cultural context. To a large extent, the shadow of slavery is still casting a reflection over the Black family (Clarke, 1991). "The Black family has not completely recovered because many factors and behaviors from the slavery experience continue today" (Williams, 1991, p. 4). Economic exploitation, racial oppression, political domination, and disfranchisement are still ever present realities in the Black experience. To understand the dynamics that are prevalent in the family today, it is necessary to understand the experiences and situations from which these dynamics were initiated. Blacks continue to experience many unique disadvantages throughout their lives (Nobles, Goddard, Cavil, & George, 1987). "The centuries of senseless cruelty and the permeation of the Black man's character with the conviction of his own hatefulness and inferiority tells a sorry tale" (Grier & Cobbs, 1980, p. 208). The lives of Blacks in America have been painful, desolate, and filled with grief, bitterness, self-hatred, rage and blind hopelessness. The process normally begins with the child and it is ultimately manifested in the adult.

> The horror carries the endorsement of centuries and the entire life-span of a nation. It is a way of life which reaches back to the beginnings of recorded time. And all the bestiality, wherever it occurs and however long it has been happening, is narrowed, focused, and refined to shine into a black child's eyes, when first he views his world. All that has ever hap-

> pened to black men and women he sees in the victims closest to him, his parents.
>
> A life is an eternity and throughout all that eternity a black child has breathed the foul air of cruelty. He has grown up to find that his spirit was crushed before he knew there was need of it. His ambition, even in their forming, showed him to have set his hand against his son. This is the desolation of black life in America (Grier & Cobbs, 1980, p. 208).

Since the so-called demise of slavery, the Black experience has been filled with many dilemmas. Only now is it apparent that a heavy burden is placed on Black children by a nation that does not want them to grow into mature men and women (Grier & Cobbs, 1980). "Persisting to this day is an attitude, shared by Black and White alike, that Blacks are inferior. This belief permeates every facet of this country and it is the etiological agent from which has developed that national sickness" (1980, p. 31). Through a conscious process transmitted by Europeans, an unconscious process by parents, daily conditioning and programming, Black children soon learn to hate and despise themselves and those closest to them.

Grier and Cobbs (1980) made the following statements about how Blacks learn to despise themselves:

> For black and white alike, the air of this nation is profused with the idea of white supremacy and everyone grows to manhood under this influence. Americans find that it is a basic part of their nationhood to despise blacks. No man who breathes this air can avoid it and black men are no exception. They are taught to hate themselves, and if at some point they discover that they are the object of hatred, they are faced with

> an additional task, nothing less, for the imperative remains that Negroes are to be despised.
>
> Thus the dynamic of black self-hatred are unique. They involve the child's awareness that all people who are black as he is are so treated by white people. Whatever hostility he mounts against white people finds little support in the weakness and the minority status of black people. As it is hopeless for him to consider righting this wrong by force, he identifies with his oppressor psychologically in an attempt to escape from his hopeless position. From his new psychologically white position, he turns on black people with aggression and hostility and hates blacks and, among the blacks, himself (pp. 198-199).

Unable to directly release their anger and frustration on the oppressive conditions of ghetto life, Blacks take out their frustration and bitterness on themselves and those closest to them—family members. The psychological forces that turn aggression inward against family members are one of the devastating features of racial and class oppression. Most colonial people display the same pattern of internalized aggression and violence against those closest to them. Violence acts against family members become an accepted and safe way to vent aggression; it is the "normal" way in which people respond (Hutchinson, 1990).

As a result of their history, Black violent offenders usually lack a sense of competence in any social role; they must develop a sense of competence before being able to relate to their family in a more "normal" manner. They have what can be referred to as a devalued self-concept, which is the product of a lifetime of social causation (Smith, 1968). This is a low sense of self-regard, in which the offenders believe they are failures, and unable to positively affect their lives. People who nurture feelings of inadequacy sometimes resort to violence as a bluff of strength to cover their low self-esteem (Star, 1983). Violent offenders may never have the opportunity to effectively interact with their environment. They may never have experienced a sense of competence in dealing with their immediate milieu, which is necessary for the development of a mature personality (White, 1959). All counselees bring the total of their experiences to the counseling setting. In all probability Blacks will continue to have these types of negative experiences in this country. As a result of these experiences, Blacks have developed a different set of values, needs, aspirations, culture, and outlook on life (Smith, 1978).

Resistance to Treatment

From conversations with counselors, many of them, both Black and white, still do therapy with Black and white clients from European and American perspectives; and believe that all people have essentially the same basic drives, motivations, and psychodynamics. There is reason to question, however, whether traditional approaches to treatment have much relevance for the Black experience—without significant modifications. It is further hypothesized that many premises upon which counseling is built, as they pertain to Blacks, may be faulty (McAdoo, 1977). Certainly, the many cultural dimensions of Blacks usually are not fully considered when working with the Black client. To be appropriate for Black families, a treatment model should clarify and demonstrate some understanding of values and behaviors considered essential to their behavioral dynamics as well as the total Black experience. The technique used must consider the client's ethnic group, culture, and race: Counselors who understand and accept this theoretical position will have little difficulty modifying their technique in ways that take into account such determinants of behavior (Lyles & Carter, 1982). Otherwise, Blacks will continue to have difficulty in interpersonal counseling relationships. Neighbors (1984) emphasized the point that Blacks were not likely to seek professional help until a problem reached the crisis stage, and were more likely to attribute their psychiatric problems to a physical problem. McKinlay (1975) suggests that the poor underutilized counseling services. Neighbors and Jackson (1984) noted that Black women are more likely to use professional help than men. Women are more likely to use both informal and formal help. Black women talk more to their informal acquaintances about their problems than men. Black men appear more isolated. Blacks as a whole are much more likely to turn to informal networks, but are more likely to seek no help at all, than other groups. It is well known that Black clients are resistive to counseling. Two of the major ways in which they are resistive are discussed below.

<u>Non self-disclosing</u>. In order for a counselor to work effectively with a client, the first requirement is verbal accessibility. This is the readiness to communicate in words about one's most important thoughts and feelings. This idea is crucial in designing the most effective plan for helping the client. Verbal accessibility or readiness to communicate is necessary for intervention (Welles, 1981). Ridley (1984) suggests that Blacks have difficulty self-disclosing: that is making the self known to other persons. The role of the therapist is to facilitate the client's willingness to explore and understand his or her feelings and actions. The client's ability to express feelings result in greater self-awareness and insight, and this newly achieved sense of the previously undisclosed self, in turn, provides the impetus for psychological growth and personal behavior change. Non self-disclosing is a barrier to therapeutic progress and, may be an indicator of further pathology. Blacks express themselves interpersonally by "playing it cool" and exhibiting a "healthy cultural paranoia." Every person is viewed as a potential enemy, and every social system is an opponent (Grier & Cobbs, 1968).

The result is a reluctance to expose their inner psychological world (Vontress, 1969).

> Many black clients and most black Americans keep their antennas out and functioning. Blacks, by nature of their survival experiences have had to be cautious about exposing themselves to people... .Many black clients refuse to or are hesitant to expose themselves because they get bad vibes from their counselors from which they conclude that the counselors cannot help them or are unwilling to help them. Second, blacks must protect themselves or get ripped off. How do we know that this is true? The answer to this question is simple. Our life experiences have dictated this truth incessantly. Therefore many clients will never expose themselves to their counselor (Smith, 1978, p. 94).

Informal networks. Many Blacks have not been able to afford counseling, and thus have not grown accustomed to using it. Blacks have, for the most part, considered counseling a luxury, being concerned with more concrete issues (food, clothing, shelter). They have always relied on a network of friends, relatives, and neighbors for help, as well as counseling and guidance, rather than counselors (McAdoo, 1977; Neighbors, 1984). The church, friends, neighbors, relatives and the extended family have always been an important part of this informal network. Factors such as discrimination and racism have led Black people to tend to rely on kin networks rather than to trust outsiders. Since counselors are usually considered to be outside this network, they are considered a threat to the confidentially of their personal thoughts, feelings, and troubles. Thus, the client may not be willing to discuss personal issues until a relationship of trust has been developed (Boyd-Franklin, 1984). While the white client may use a counselor, the Black client may turn to their own family or extended family in times of crisis (McAdoo,

1977). In many cases, the client either finds no outside sources of help or those that are available are viewed as unsympathetic to the minority experience. Blacks usually have a distrust of counselors (Sager & Braboy, 1970). The client will usually resist, especially when asked to come involuntarily (Foley, 1975; Sager & Braboy, 1970; McAdoo, 1977; Boyd, 1977).

Treatment Model

Most violent offenders have a problem with anger, but the Black offender's anger arises from a different source. In Blacks, it is not necessarily internal pathology that leads to anger and frustration, causing one to lash out at family members. Black offenders' anger arises out of the socio-historical and present context in which they exist, and from which they have developed. The Black individual and family have undergone significant trauma in this country. Today, they continue to undergo trauma on a daily basis. This has resulted in the present conditions of the Black family. Both male and female are frustrated at their conditions. This causes a great deal of anger. Because of frustration and anger at a racist, discriminatory, prejudice and bigoted society; this anger and frustration is turned inward, ventilated, and expressed within the family situation. It must be noted here that much of this violence in the family arises out of a threatened loss or perceived lack of power that relates in part to the socio-historical context out of which the family has developed. To some extent racism has caused Blacks to have a sense of powerlessness, lack of control, and impotence. They see themselves as being able to control very little in their environment. When they find that they cannot control their home situation, it becomes unbearable, and leads to violence in domestic relations. Many males especially perceive a threatened loss of power, and react to sustain that power. For Blacks the family remains the place where most frustration and anger are released. The frustration and anger that arises out of this context cause the violent activity that is witnessed in the family today. In many cases, Blacks are frustrated in childhood because of inadequate parenting; they are frustrated in the school system because of an inadequate system; they are frustrated in the job market because of inadequate job opportunities, and are frustrated generally because of a racist society. In fact, negative stereotypes are held about Blacks around the world. The Black offender faces in this society what can be conceptualized as a pathological triangle: a racist society, racist employer, and a negative family situation that results from the first two factors (see Figure 1). This pathological triangle keeps Blacks going around in circles, getting caught up in their own deteriorated state, and unable to alleviate their basic pathological condition. This situation has been affecting the Black family for many generations; what we are witnessing today, in terms of family violence, is a manifestation of the buildup of intergenerational pathology.

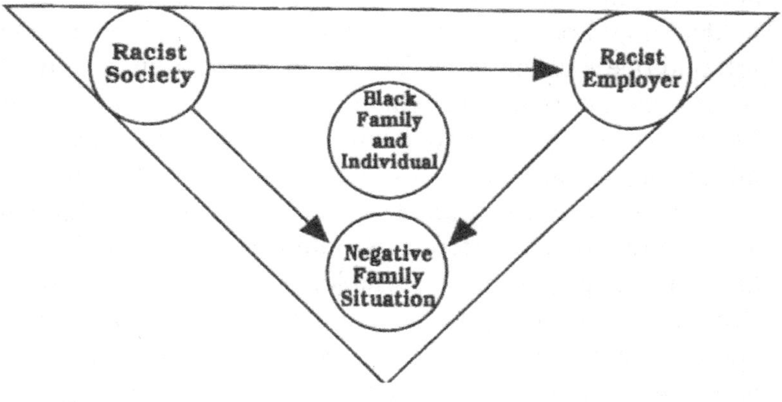

Figure 1. The Pathological triangle of the Black violent offender and family.

After reviewing the historical and present conditions of the Black family, and some natural resistances on the part of the Black offender, the following model evolves as one that is most appropriate in counseling with the violent offender in Black domestic relations. It will be necessary to help the offender to begin to understand this present and socio-historical context in which the family exists. The impact of this situation on the family must be understood by the offender. It will be helpful to begin by having the offender to read books on the socio-historical context and present context of the Black family. This material should be discussed for its relevance to the offender's situation. The counselor must help the offender to develop the necessary competence in negotiating with the environment: that is, how to cope with problems and how to control events and not be controlled by them (Breton, 1981). The counselor should help the individual learn conflict resolution. The offender must be helped to understand and not feel demoralized over situations that cannot be immediately changed. He or she should be helped to realize that it is appropriate to feel dissatisfied with the present situation, but must feel good about who one is at all times, and keep exerting effort for change. The offender should be helped to feel positive, and believe in one's self and one's capabilities. The offender must understand the socio-cultural context in which he or she exists (see Figure 2). He or she should understand that if one has themselves under control, and understand what they can and cannot control, the variables in Figure 2 are more easily manipulated and controlled. The offender should be helped to understand how to manipulate these variables within the socio-cultural context for the purpose of maximizing change for one's self and for the community. The limit of this socio-cultural context must be interpreted to the offender, giving him or her a better understanding of this context in which one must function. The offender must also develop self-control and learn to set limits on one's behavior. This means that the person can then have greater control over his or her life. The offender

Figure 2. The socio-cultural context of an African-American individual or family.

must learn to appropriately cope, and begin to take the necessary control over one's personal space. Find more constructive alternatives to hitting (Star, 1983), and attain greater facility over thoughts and feelings through verbal interchange. Most important, the offender must learn to take responsibility for his or her actions. The offender must identify external and internal impediments and solutions to why he or she does not seem to progress (Calia, 1966).

By going through such a process, the offender will develop a deeper more insightful level of consciousness and awareness. The objective here is more to develop the offender's conscious level rather than immediate behavior change. Though, it will be necessary to get some control over the negative behaviors immediately. Developing one's conscious level is more important on a long-term basis because, by doing so a more permanent behavior change can occur. It will take a lengthy period of developing one's conscious level before permanent behavior change can occur. In achieving this type of conscious development, rather than focusing on immediate behavior change, the offender is better able to deal with future family problems.

Conclusion

The pathological condition of the Black family arises out of an entrenched socio-historical and present-day situation. It is necessary to understand these situations before understanding the violence that takes place within the Black family, and the subsequent nature of the violent offender. The socio-historical and present-day conditions of the family must be taken into account before the development of an adequate model for counseling the violent family offender. It is concluded that because of the traumatic situation to which Black offenders have been exposed; they have turned their anger inward toward the family, this results in an abnormal amount of violence in the family. It is suggested that it is possible to treat violent Black offenders by helping them to learn to better negotiate their environment. That includes learning what one can and cannot control, and beginning to take some responsibility for one's behavior. It is proposed that this technique be used in such a manner as to help the offender to develop his or her level of consciousness in relationship to the family. This will aid in the ability of the offender to deal with any future problems encountered in the family.

References

Boyd, N. (1977). Black families in therapy: A study of clinicians' perceptions. Psychiatric Spectator, 41, 21-25.

Boyd-Franklin, N. (1984). Issues in family therapy with Black families. Clinical Psychologist, 37, 54-58.

Breton, M. (1981). Remobilization of abusive parents. Social Work, 26, 19-22.

Calia, V. (1966). The culturally deprived client: A reformulation of the counselor's role. Journal of Counseling Psychology, 13, 100-105.

Clarke, J.H. (1991). Notes for an African world revolution: Africans at the crossroads. Trenton, New Jersey: Africa World Press, Inc.

Foley, V. (1975). Family therapy with Black disadvantaged families: Some observations on roles, communications, and techniques. Journal of Marriage and Family, 1, 29-38.

Green, M.A. (1975). Impact of slavery on the Black family: Social, political, and economic. Journal of Afro-American Issues, 3, 343-356.

Grier, W.H., & Cobbs, P.M. (1980). Black Rage. New York: Basic Books, Inc., Publishers.

Hutchinson, E.O. (1990). The mugging of Black America. Chicago: African American Images.

Holtz, H., & Furniss, K.K. (1991, March). Getting involved: Health care workers and domestic violence. USA Today, pp. 88-89.

Jones, L.C. (1993, March). Why are we beating our children? Ebony, pp. 80-82.

Landes, B., Siegel, A., & Foster, C.D. (1993). Domestic violence: No longer behind the curtain. Wylie, Texas: Information Plus.

Lyles, M.R., & Carter J.H. (1982). Myths and strengths of the Black family: A historical and sociological contribution to family therapy. Journal of the National Medical Association, 74, 1119-1123.

McAdoo, H. (1977). Family therapy in the Black community. American Journal of Orthopsychiatry, 47, 75-79.

McKinlay, J. (1975). The help Seeking behavior of the poor. In J. Kosa & I. Zola (Eds.), Poverty and health: A sociological analysis (2nd ed., pp. 224-273). Cambridge Massachusetts: Harvard University Press.

Neighbors, H.W. (1984). Professional help use among Black Americans: Implications for unmet needs. American Journal of Community Psychology, 12, 551-565.

Neighbors, H.W., & Jackson, J.S. (1984). The use of informal and formal help: Four patterns of illness behavior in the Black community. American Journal of Community Psychology, 12, 629-644.

Nobles, W.W., Goddard, L.L., Cavil, W.E., & George P.Y. (1987). African American families: Issues, insights, and directions. Oakland, California: Black Family Institute Publication.

Ridley, C.R. (1984). Clinical treatment of the non-disclosing Black client: A therapeutic paradox. American Psychologist, 39, 1234-1244.

Smith, M.B. (1968). Competence and socialization. In John Clausen (Ed.), Socialization and society (pp. 278-288). Boston: Little Brown and Company.

Smith, W. (1978). Black perspectives on counseling. In G. Waltz & L. Benjamin (Eds.), Transcultural counseling: Needs, programs and techniques (pp. 83-110). New York: Human Science Press.

Star, B. (1983). Helping the abuser: Intervening effectively in family violence. New York: Family Service Association of America.

Vontress, C. (1969). Cultural barriers in the counseling relationship. Personnel and Guidance Journal, 48, 11-17.

Welles, S.J. (1981). A model of therapy with abusive and neglected families. Social Work, 26, 113-119.

White, R.W. (1959, September). Motivation reconsidered: The concept of competence. Psychological Review, 66, 233-297.

Williams, R. (1991). They stole it but you must return it. New York: Hema Publishing.

Chapter 12

Psycho-Educational Model for Counseling African American Children

---

Introduction

There is no question that society leaves an indelible mark on many African American children. Although racism is a problem for many African American children, some escape many of the negative effects of this process. Many are able to creatively deal with it in such a way as to achieve in the face of overwhelming odds. It is not necessary to prove here that racism exists in America, or that this racism has a tremendous impact on the youth. This chapter does not set out to prove these facts because they are axiomatic. It is known that the problems of some African American children are rooted in oppression, lack of opportunity, violated human freedom, and ethnocentrism (Ivey, Ivey, & Simek-Morgan, 1993; Kunjufu, 1984; Lee, 1993; Lee & Richardson, 1991; Frankllin, 1989).

Counteracting negativity. In this chapter, it will be demonstrated how to work with African American children in counseling who have been affected by racism, and how parents and counselors can counteract the negativity imposed by society. It is necessary to train children in such a manner as to combat racism. The question in this chapter is: how does one work with an African American child in such a manner as to instill self-esteem and a positive self-concept? What factors will contribute to the development of a positive self-concept and self-identity?

The need to unite and work collectively. The future of African Americans will lie in what the group is able to accomplish, and not in what a few individuals within the group will be able to accomplish. Therefore, it will be necessary for children to focus on the community as a whole rather than what they can accomplish for and by themselves. Unity will help to combat racism (Kunjufu, 1991; Shakari, 1991; Woodson, 1990). Children must realize that they will need to fight this negativity individually and collectively. Children must be able to see their future from this frame-of-reference. The child must learn what racism is, what it does to a group of people affected by it, and how to overcome as well as work toward its alleviation. The child is a part of the family, the family is a part of the larger community, and the community is a part of the society. It should be apparent that African American children are surrounded by a society that is essentially racist, one that devalues many of the accomplishments of African Americans (Franklin, 1989; Johnson & White, 1991; Murray, Smith, & West, 1989). It is no wonder that many children develop a low sense of self-esteem and self-concept. It is surprising that a preponderance of African American children are not dysfunctional or deficit ridden (Greene, 1992). It must be recognized that problems exist in the development of children, and that it is necessary to analyze why and how these problems are perpetuated (Kunjufu, 1984).

Using adaptive strategies. Children must be taught values that will make themselves and the group strong, as well as those values that will help them to overcome the racist ideas already imposed by some whose goals are to create and maintain a racist society. African American children may be found in state, county, and other psychiatric health care facilities at a rate 75% higher than their European-American counterparts. It has also been suggested that 10 to 25% are at significant risk for developing clinical depression during their childhood (Edelman, 1985). There is much depression, anger, and despair among African American children (Franklin, 1989). They must use a variety of adaptive strategies to cope with racism and sequels of racial discrimination. Many European Americans verbalize the idea that this is a just society, and the reason African Americans are not in better positions is their own deficiencies. In addition, European Americans could bring about consequences as a result of their perceptions. This view causes further negative evaluations, and leads to more subtle and unsubtle forms of racism (Crosby, Bromley, & Saxe, 1980; Gaertner & Dovidio, 1981; Gaertner & McLaughlin, 1983; McConahay & Hough, 1976).

How racism turns to self-hatred. While it is not necessary to establish that racism exists, it is necessary to demonstrate how African American children come to be affected by racism. What a person thinks of himself or herself is in many ways dependent upon how one is perceived by others. Mead (1934), Cooley (1956), Sullivan (1953), Erikson (1968), and Essien-Udom (1962) suggest that self-identity and self-concept comes through interaction with other members of the society; this includes all significant others, and some not so significant. The two basic proponents of this idea were Cooley (1956) and Mead (1934). Mead (1934) suggests that a sense of self was developed and molded from taking on the attitudes, values, and definitions of others toward them. When a person is a member of society, its values, goals, attitudes, and norms become one's own. Cooley (1956) compares the process of developing a self-concept to looking in a mirror. The person sees a reflection in the mirror and evaluates this appearance; similarly, individuals will judge their own appearance by the way other persons indicate they view them. The social context is very important for the development of the self-concept. It is likely that an African American child will develop a negative self–concept from everyday exposure to society. Black children constantly receive negative messages telling them that they are inferior, and because of this they are relegated to an inferior position in society. Many children then try to approximate European American ideals, rejecting themselves and others like them.

Having developed a self-concept from the social context, children see themselves in a negative light. The child may then develop a preference for white things (Clark & Clark, 1947; Morland, 1962; Goodman, 1952) and express resentment and hostility toward his/her own group. Some African American children tend to resent many of their physical characteristics. This causes some negative behaviors on the part of the child. There is much maladjustment (Rainwater, 1967; Boykin, 1957), rejection of other African Americans (Yarrow, 1958), and a host of other emotional problems. Many studies indicate that African American children develop self-hatred as a result of being indoctrinated into this culture. Among these studies are the famous studies done by Clark and Clark (1950), in which children showed a preference for lighter-skin dolls.

> African American children face the task of learning to be bicultural in an antagonistic environment. To succeed at this task, they must learn to imitate the dominant culture whether they accept its values or not. This is complicated by the dominant culture's insidious devaluation of person of color. African American children thus face the realistic consequences of a legacy of racial discrimination, just as their parents do (Greene, 1962, p. 65).

It is possible for counselors, parents, family, and community to negate the negative effects of the wider socio-cultural context and lead to the development of a healthier self-concept in African American children. Children can develop a positive self-concept under certain conditions. They only need a sense of unity as a people, group identification, Black consciousness and pride. Imposed against the community, this can serve as a filter against the harmful inputs from the larger society. This would lead individuals to feel better about who they are, what they are like, where they fit in the world, their worth and value (Johnson & White, 1991; Barnes, 1991).

The Psycho-Educational Model

Rather than counseling alone, this model combines counseling and education. It is believed that many African American problems are derived from lack of employment, lack of opportunity, racism, discrimination, prejudice, etc. These problems are not of an individual pathology, but perhaps develop from a society that is unfair and unequal in the amount of opportunity offered to most African American members (Franklin, 1989; Jackson, 1983; Gilbert & Willis, 1994; Madhubuti, 1990). Therefore an individual pathology approach is not taken here, but one that seeks to educate the child about racism in this country and the history of Africans in the world, as well as how this history affects the present state of Africans all over the world. The child is asked questions and is given feedback. Issues are placed within a societal context, showing individuals how they are affected by society. Traditionally, what occurred in the African community (in the part where most African Americans came from) was group focused. This model seeks to teach children about their history, how to develop self-esteem, and to overcome and alleviate the effects of racism. It is more fitting to use this model, since most of these problems are considered to be generated by a racist society, rather than individually induced psychopathology (Jackson, 1983; Gilbert & Willis,

1994). By counselors adhering to such a model, many advanced psychological problems seen in adulthood can be eliminated. The goal should be a positive self concept through development of one's self- and racial-identity.

Children should be helped to understand who they are, what they are all about, and where they came from. These children must be helped to build their self-esteem, feel good about themselves (Jones, 1991), build their identity with this African culture, and improve their self-image. They need to be given an outlook that is consistent with their culture. Children should analyze images, literature, history, etc., from an African-centered perspective. They should read and discuss materials with an African-centered frame-of-reference and engage in activities such as these that will promote racial identity, pride in culture, and cultural awareness (Lee, 1989). This will happen simply by being exposed to this type of cultural materials. Many African American have accepted a European American frame-of-reference since being in this country. There is a need to reorient themselves to their own standards of beauty and culture. The greatest challenge for children is to develop positive self-images (Kunjufu, 1984). They must learn to feel better about their characteristics, and to be group oriented. Institutional leaders must define new values, goals, norms about what is good and desirable, from the standpoint of the groups own interest and conditions of existence. Practicing self-determination will help lead to a positive self-concept. It is necessary to emphasize group solidarity, cohesion, and a sense that being an African American has positive value. The counselor should provide a sense of purpose, a sense of an ideology, and an understanding of the realities of racism (Jones, 1991). This is necessary to transmit purpose to the next generation: African people have a common history, identity, and destiny. To identify with African culture, create a sense of community, togetherness, and development of aesthetic norms. Through a process of developing group solidarity, self-determination, and definition (development of Black norms), children can begin to arrive at their potential. This should facilitate and enhance the development of the self-concept in African American children. If parents are mis-oriented, obviously they will need some help in relating to and helping children to maximize their educational, social and psychological potential. The counselor must then help parents to achieve certain objectives that are necessary for this development. Counselors bear the major responsibility, because they will have to fill the void left vacant by some parents. Sometimes parents can provide what is necessary with a little assistance. Counselors will have a dual role—to work with both parents and children, providing counseling to children, and assistance to many parents in helping children to develop correct ways of functioning. The more of these things counselors are able to assist parents in providing, the fewer counselors will need to provide directly to the child. There is some overlap between the role of educator, counselor and parent, as implied in Table 1. The parent is educator and counselor; the counselor is an educator, and at times a parent; and the educator is a counselor, and at times serves *in loco parentis*.

Role of the counselor. In counseling with African American children one must have an appreciation of the dynamics of culture, and the societal forces that impinge upon the mental health and well-being of African American children (Lee, 1991). The goal of counseling African American children should be maximum rather than optimum mental health. Counseling should be preventive rather than remedial. Children should be helped to understand that there is a need to contribute to the system of which they are a part, and that they must be prepared to make changes within this system. Children need to have ethnic awareness, identity and pride. They need to improve their self-concept, self-worth, self-confidence, self-image, and to gain a sense of mastery of their environment and life (Lee, 1989; Johnson & White,

Table 1
The Basic Elements in The Psycho-Educational Model

A TRICHOTOMY OF THE PSYCHO-EDUCATIONAL MODEL

COUNSELING

HELP CHILDREN TO:

1.) Understand that there is a need, and that they must be prepared to change as well as contribute to the system of which they are a part.

2.) Develop ethnic awareness, identity and pride.

3.) Improve self-concept, self-worth, self-confidence, self-image, and gain a sense of mastery.

4.) Develop self-awareness and environmentally adaptive behaviors that lead to psychological well-being.

5.) Increase awareness of African-American culture.

6.) Raise conscious level and self-expectation level.

7.) Understand the outside world's messages and how to tell when message are true.

8.) Develop "racial socialization" skills.

9.) To survive in a racist society.

10.) Develop conscious level and self-control.

11.) See themselves as adequate and desirable as love objects.

12.) Develop purpose and direction.

13.) Understand racism.

SUPPORTIVE PARENTS

HELP CHILDREN TO:

1.) Learn who they are, and who and what oppresses them.

2.) Learn positive values and develop competence and self-esteem.

3.) Develop: by serving as a role model.

4.) Make decisions that are in their best interest.

5.) Develop a concept of community.

6.) Understand their position in the world.

7.) Experience diversity.

8.) Learn that physical characteristics are less important than how one thinks.

9.) Be self motivated.

10.) Communicate openly.

11.) Associate with positive people and do positive things.

12.) Learn what is right and what is wrong.

13.) Be positive and have a sense of direction.

14.) Overcome their mistakes.

15.) Understand their own behavior.

16.) Properly conceptualize the environment.

EDUCATION

HELP CHILDREN TO:

1.) Pursue, explore, and develop potential.

2.) Think for themselves.

3.) Maintain curiosity and enthusiasm

4.) Learn biculturalism without losing a sense of themselves.

5. Examine own strengths and liabilities.

6. Examine total support system.

7.) Develop interaction and socialization skills

8.) Understand history.

9.) Understand who they are, what they are all about, and where they came from.

10.) Promote their own racial-identity, pride in culture, and cultural awareness.

11.) Develop their own standards of beauty and culture.

1991; Barnes, 1991). It is necessary for counselors to promote self-awareness, and environmentally adaptive behaviors that lead to psychological well-being. Counselors should attempt to heighten awareness, helping children to understand certain aspects of African American culture. It is important to raise their conscious level and self-expectation levels. The counselor should, "Help the child understand the outside world's messages and how to tell when those messages are true" (Greene, 1992, p.68). Besides raising their conscious level, they should be helped to learn about as many different cultural values as possible, without losing a sense of themselves and their own culture. They should discuss and share derivatives of African American cultural values and practices, as well as pride in African culture. Counselors must work with parents to encourage positive "racial socialization" (Greene, 1992). Greene (1992) uses the term "racial socialization" synonymously with what is here referred to as "racial education." This is the teaching of socialization skills in dealing with racism; learning to cope with the negativity that exist within society. In many situations, parents do not teach these skills. Children should receive respect (Lee, 1989), attention, affection, and discipline from their parents; the counselor should assist parents in providing these things. Children should benefit from counselors helping them learn how to survive in a negative society (1989). They should help these children to develop their conscious level and self-control. Counselors should help parents to become conscious of how they interact with the child. The counselor should help children to examine their strengths, liabilities and total support system. Self-esteem and self-concept are the two variables most affected by this negativity. It would greatly benefit children for counselors to help them develop identity, purpose, and direction. It is necessary for counselors to assist in the development of identity and cooperativeness if children are to become fully functional.

It is suggested that counselors use whatever traditional methods at their disposal to achieve these objectives: take home assignments and activities, group activities, movies, videos, tapes, individual counseling, distribution of reading material, and other personal contacts should be utilized (Lee, 1989; Johnson & White, 1991). Every available opportunity should be used for this purpose.

Role of the parents. Parents must first feel good about themselves before they can help to promote positive mental health in children. The author is suggesting that these parents have been conditioned by the system, and thus have been affected by certain types of negativity; many of these parents have been conditioned by the system to the extent that they are confused about their identity. If parents are confused, they cannot serve as adequate role models for their children. The parents will need to overcome their own conditioning before they can assist the children with their issues. Counselors must first help some parents to develop the skills and awareness to work with their own children. At the same time parents should teach their children who they are, other positive values; and help to develop a healthy self-esteem, positive self-image, self-worth, personal competence and healthy self-concept (Kunjufu, 1984; Franklin, 1989). They should serve as positive role models, while enabling them to make decisions that are in their best interest. It is necessary to provide a sense of self, self-acceptance and self-identity. If parents teach self-awareness it will overcome self-hatred. Parents should teach them a realistic view of their self-esteem, as well as how to sustain this self-esteem (Johnson & White, 1991). They should teach a concept of group or "weness" as opposed to "I": a concept of community instead of individual. Children should be given a solid sense of competence and a sturdy sense of self. Children should be provided with an understanding of contemporary problems that confront African Americans and other Africans. It is important for parents to help them to understand their place in the world, and to appreciate African American heritage.

In addition to the above, parents must provide an array of diversified experiences to help develop talents, acquire knowledge and skills sufficient for their continued development. Children should be helped to maintain curiosity and enthusiasm: to understand that physical characteristics are less important than how one thinks; provide motivation and help to be self-motivated; and taught to think for themselves. It is necessary for parents to set a strong foundation for children's future development and provide positive relationships. Children should always be taught a lesson—even in many forms of play. It is important to provide children with the knowledge to become more conscious in their daily lives of what is around them. Parents should always communicate with the child at every available opportunity, making every effort to understand the child's behavior. It is important for children to learn to associate with positive people and do positive things. Children should develop a conscience, know what is right, and what is wrong. It is important not to denigrate children by constantly bombarding them with negatives. Parents should always maintain a sense of direction for the children and themselves. If possible, facilitate the child's involvement in things in which they demonstrate some potential. If children fail, help them to understand why, and how to overcome their mistakes.

This model is designed for counselors, whom must first be trained by consciously aware African American institutional leaders and professionals: the particular field of the trainer does not matter—only the ability to provide the necessary training. Europeans who are trained to understand African American culture and values should have no problems in providing the necessary training.

Counselors can best help parents by relating to both children and their parents as a unit. The counselor can also hold group meetings and activities, give parents assignments, distribute reading material and give suggested reading material, movies, videos, tapes, etc. The overall objective of the counselor will be simply to raise the conscious level of the parents to facilitate the development of their children. There will be resistance on the part of the parents, which is simply a natural process of inertia and many years of conditioning. This will be a slow process, and parents will have to be worked with until they develop the appropriate understanding in order for them to move to a higher level of parenting.

How Counselor's Adherence to This Model Will Benefit Children

Facilitating a child's development in the following broad areas will help the child to acquire the necessary skills to overcome the above mentioned negativity. These are just a few of the basic areas in which sufficient development will help the child to grow and overcome an adverse environment. It is most essential that a child understands history, develops a sense of self, and develops an awareness of African American culture (Barnes, 1991; Johnson & White, 1991).

History. If children understand their history they will be able to attack this negativity at its roots wherever it exists. If children do not know their past, they have no understanding of the present, and have no future (Rodney, 1981). If they do not understand what happened in 1492, it will be difficult to understand what happened in 2002. It is very important to understand the part that African Americans have played on the world scene, not just after reaching the shores of America, but throughout antiquity (Woodson, 1990; Williams, 1987; Clarke, 1991). Children must understand that there were great scholars on the scene in African antiquity that developed many techniques that are presently being utilized in science and industry. By understanding the contributions of the Black race in the past, African American children can begin to understand and appreciate their own capabilities (Clarke, 1991). On the basis of much of today's media coverage, children can easily get the idea that African Americans are only good at sports and music. Since many African American children are aware that only a few will be successful at sports and music, they conclude that the only other alternative is to push drugs, and function in an underground illegal economy. This is rather twisted logic, but the logic that some African American children follow.

A sense of history will help to produce self-esteem, self-worth, dignity, purpose and meaning in the minds of African American children. Without this, they are likely to feel useless, hopeless and without purpose; feeling that African Americans have never played a major role in contributing to world civilization, and have no ability to function in that way. J. A. Rogers (1972) noted that, "… it is undeniable that a knowledge of one's ancestors does have a certain psychological value, especially if such ancestors were worthy" (p. 8). This would be an inspiration, especially for the youth of that culture. Knowing history can help one to understand what African Americans have contributed to world civilization (Williams, 1987; Woodson, 1990; Clarke, 1991). If studied adequately, one will not only understand the contributions but also will understand exactly why, where, and how African Americans were placed in the position they are in today. Understanding history will also enable them to figure out what needs to be done to alleviate their present difficulties (Clarke, 1991).

Sense of self. Self-esteem, self-identity, self-concept, pride in self, and in the group are all indications of the level of one's sense of self (Jones, 1991). It is necessary to build a child's sense of self as much as possible. A healthy sense of self helps children to be in a better position to learn and develop. Children who have a strong self-concept are better equipped to survive racism. African Americans must develop a sense of who, where, and what they are before they can go on to improve life for themselves. African American identity has been lost in the diffusion with American culture (Gilbert, Hughley, & Willis, 1994). It is felt by the author that, as a result of playing a subordinate role in the American culture for such an extensive period, many African American have begun to lack clarity regarding their identity. They strive to imitate European Americans but have difficulty being accepted. They have been conditioned to not like themselves. They have been in this culture for such an extensive period that they have, in most cases, lost much of their "Afrocentricity" (1994). If children do not know who they are, they will have no respect for themselves, and have no respect for or identify with other Black people and culture (Barnes, 1989).

<u>Develop an awareness of Black culture</u>. African American children must develop an awareness of their culture. African Americans were not allowed to practice this culture for much of history. At this point, over the generations, most of them have lost touch with this culture. Children must be taught to practice and appreciate their culture. They should learn the values, norms, and habits of African culture. They must learn to appreciate all African physical characteristics. Children should identify with Black culture, and one's own racial characteristics: hair, eyes, nose, lips, etc. It is important to learn all about the solar system (system of the planets), but it is just as important to learn about the "soul-ar system" (the essence of Black folk and their environment).

Conclusion

Many African American children have problems because of racism, prejudice and discrimination resulting in lack of opportunity; but many of them have problems for other reasons. It should not be overlooked, for example, that Black communities have failed to come together in unity, consolidate resources, network, and provide mutual support to one another; there has been a failure to build African American communities. This in itself has caused many children to be denied an equal opportunity. The problems began from lack of opportunities that had roots in the African American's early history in this country. Some have in the past, but cannot continue to attribute the majority of problems to this history or to other individuals. If children are to grow and develop, they must be given a rich legacy from which to do so. Part of the counseling process must teach the present generation of youth to get prepared to provide this legacy. In this way future generations can avoid many of the problems of present and past generations. To unify and consolidate resources is one of the many preventive solutions for future generations. If children can be taught skills to fortify them against racism, and can develop their own communities, they can go on to lead productive lives. This model would help to alleviate the problems of African American children, whether the issue is racism or failure to unite as a people.

References

Barnes, E.J. (1991). The Black community as the source of positive self-concept for Black children: A theoretical perspective. In R. Jones (Ed.), Black psychology (pp. 667-692). Berkeley, California: Cobb & Henry.

Boykin, L.L. (1957). The adjustment of 2,078 Negro students. Journal of Negro Education, 26, 75-79.

Clark, K.B., & Clark, M.P. (1947). Racial identification and prejudice in Negro children. In T.M. Newcomb & E.L. Hartley (Eds.), Readings in social psychology (pp. 169-178). New York: Holt, Rinehart & Winston.

Clarke, J.H. (1991). Notes for an African world revolution. Trenton, New Jersey: African World Press.

Cooley, C.H. (1956). Human nature and the social order. New York: Free Press.

Crosby, F., Bromley, S., & Saxe, L. (1980). Recent unobtrusive studies of Black and white discrimination and prejudice: A literature review. Psychological Bulletin, 87, 546-563.

Edelman, M.W. (1985). The sea is so wide and my boat is so small: Problems facing Black children today. In H. McAdoo & J. McAdoo (Eds.), Black children: social, educational and parental environments (pp. 72-82). Newbury Park, California: Sage.

Erikson, E.H. (1968). Identity, youth and crisis. New York: Norton.

Essien-Udom, E.U. (1962). Black nationalism. New York: Dell.

Franklin, A.J. (1989).Therapeutic interventions with urban Black adolescents. In R. Jones (Ed.), Black adolescents (pp. 209-337). Berkeley, California: Cobb & Henry.

Gaertner, S.L., & Dovidio, J.F. (1981). Racism among the well-intended. In J. Bermingham & E. Clausen (Eds.), Racism, pluralism, and public policy: A search for equality (pp. 208-222). Boston: G K Hall.

Gaertner, S.L., & McLaughin, J.P. (1983). Racial stereotypes: Association and ascriptions of positive and negative characteristics. Social Psychology Quarterly, 46, 23-30.

Gilbert, N.L., Hughley, E., & Willis, J.T. (1994). Freeing the African-American's mind. Matteson, Illinois: Behavioral Systems Consultants Publications.

Gilbert, N.L., & Willis, J.T. (1994). An alternative conceptual model for diagnosing African Americans in psychotherapy. In N. Gilbert, E. Hughley & J. Willis (Eds.), Freeing the African-American's mind (pp. 209-231). Matteson, Illinois: Behavioral Systems Consultants Publications.

Goodman, M.E. (1952). Race awareness in young children. Cambridge, MA: Harper.

Greene, B.A. (1992). Racial socialization as a tool in psychotherapy with African American children. In L. Vargas & J. Koss-Chioino (Eds.), Working with culture (pp. 63-81). San Francisco: Jossey-Bass.

Grier, W.H., & Cobbs, P.M. (1980). Black rage. New York: Basic Books.

Ivey, A., Ivey, B., & Simek-Morgan, L. (1993). Counseling and psychotherapy: A multicultural perspective (3rd ed.). Boston: Allyn & Bacon.

Jackson, A.M. (1983). A theoretical model for the practice of psychotherapy with Black populations. The Journal of Black Psychology, 10, 19-27.

Johnson, J.A., & White, J.L. (1991). Awareness, pride and identity: A positive educational strategy for Black youth. In R. Jones (Ed.), Black psychology (pp. 409-418). Berkeley, California: Cobb & Henry.

Jones, R. (1991). Black psychology. Berkeley, CA: Cobb & Henry.

Kunjufu, J. (1984). Developing positive self-images and discipline in Black children. Chicago: African-American Images.

Kunjufu, J. (1991). Black economics. Chicago: African-American Images.

Lee, C.C. (1989). Counseling the Black adolescent: Critical roles and functions for counseling professionals. In R. Jones (Ed.), Black adolescents (pp. 293-308). Berkeley: Cobb & Henry.

Lee, C.C. (1991). Counseling African Americans: From theory to practice. In R. Jones (Ed.), Black psychology (pp. 559-576). Berkeley: Cobb & Henry.

Lee, C.C. (Ed.). (1993). Counseling for diversity: A guide for school counselors and related professionals. Boston: Allyn & Bacon.

Lee, C.C., & Richardson, B.L. (1991). Multicultural issues in counseling: New approaches to diversity. Alexandria, VA: American Association for Counseling and Development.

Madhubuti, H. (1990). Black men. Chicago: Third World Press.

McConahay, J.B., & Hough, J.C. (1976). Symbolic racism. Journal of Social Issues, 32, 23-45.

Mead, G.H. (1934). Mind, self, and society. Chicago: University of Chicago Press.

Morland, J.K. (1962). A comparison of race awareness in northern and southern children. American Journal of Orthopsychiatry, 36, 22-31.

Murray, C.B., Smith, S.N., & West, E.H. (1989). Comparative personality development in adolescence: A critique. In R. Jones (Ed.), Black adolescents (pp. 49-62). Berkeley, California: Cobb & Henry.

Rainwater, L. (1967). Crucible of identity: The Negro lower class family. In T. Parsons & K.B. Clark (Eds.), The Negro American (pp. 160-204). Boston: Beacon Press.

Rodney, W. (1981). How Europe underdeveloped Africa. Washington, DC: Howard University Press.

Rogers, J.A. (1972). World's greatest men of color (Vol. 1). New York: MacMillan Publishing Co., Inc.

Shakari, B.A. (1991). Tribalism, mysticism, primitivism and the rise of genocide against the African world. Chicago: Shakari Publications.

Sullivan, H.S. (1953). The interpersonal theory of psychiatry. New York: Norton.

Williams, C. (1987). The destruction of Black civilization. Chicago: Third World Press.

Woodson, C.G. (1990). The mis-education of the Negro. Trenton, NJ: Africa World Press.

Yarrow, M.R. (1958). Interpersonal dynamics in a desegregation process. Journal of Social Issues, 14, 3-63.

PART V

THE FUTURE

Preliminary Comments

This book would not be complete without consideration being given to the future of the African American family. We have before us a choice to begin to work on improving our family situation or to step into that void which is destined for destruction without change or consequence.

Chapter 13 indicates that if the African American family is to survive into the twenty-first century while remaining intact, some fundamental changes in its basic structure, dynamics, and relationship patterns will need to be changed. The African American family began its decline in pre-slavery, over 10,000 years ago, eventually leading to the conditions of today, where it is plagued with many different problems that had their origin in slavery. To improve the conditions of African American men and women, they will need to first arrive at a more positive concept of who they are by understanding their history, and where they came from. They will need to then work on improving relationships between family members, as well as relationships with community agencies and institutions.

Chapter 14 is a summary of the book, calling for African American families to unite and realize that much damage has been done for which many individuals carry emotional baggage. They will need to seek help from someone whom they feel they can trust in order to rid themselves of this emotional baggage. The decision to seek help when difficulties arise is a positive step toward improving one's self and one's family.

Chapter 13

A Functional African American Family Model for the Twenty-First Century and Beyond

If the African American family is to continue to survive, thrive, and cope successfully into the twenty-first century, it must begin to improve in its functioning. The family is plagued with various problems of one kind or another: Nearly half of all families are headed by women, and most of them are considered to have poverty status; 40 to 50 percent of which are teenage mothers. This makes it difficult to provide the nurturing that young children in these families need. Children are not being trained to assume appropriate roles in an increasingly automated, highly-technical, and computerized society. Moreover, children must be trained in the basics of how to promote Black culture and the Black race in general, and how to assure its continuous development. Otherwise, a large percentage of children will continue to drop out of school, thus perpetuating and assuring that successive generations will be no better off than previous generations.

This chapter was presented at the Annual Conference of the African American Studies program at Olive-Harvey College, Chicago, Illinois, in April 1988.

Important Considerations in Developing a Family Model

Difficulty in deciding on a model. It is difficult to talk about a model for the family in the twenty-first century or at any other time, since it will undoubtedly continue to include all of the various models and alternatives that presently exist today and that have existed in the past. The family lives in the midst of Western culture and will continue to adapt to its many attributes. The Western society has adopted many models and alternatives which do not seem to be changing. Since African Americans living in Western society tend, in most instances, to imitate the larger culture, we will continue to utilize the many different models and alternatives that exist within the larger culture.

Western society still clings to the nuclear family type as its most ideal model. It is proposed that we continue to utilize the nuclear family model as the predominant model, but with some changes in the way the members play their roles and carry out their relationships with the agencies and institutions within the community and the larger society. The nuclear family model seems to be functional in many respects for Western society.

Blacks in Africa and the early years in the United States utilized an extended family model because of their beliefs and customs. It is debatable how practical the extended family model will be for the twenty-first century, due to geographic mobility and changes that families will undergo both now and in the future. Again, it is suggested that the nuclear family model may be most practical for Western society because of the conditions that exist, but it may not be the best family model for some other societies that exist under different conditions.

Defining and carrying out roles. Today, we have family models such as cohabitation, single-parent, nuclear, extended, and many other alternatives. It does not matter what model is adopted by the family. Certainly, the most important consideration, regardless of the adopted model, is that we need to concentrate on defining the roles that are to exist, and how to appropriately carry out these roles in the most efficient, effective, wholesome, and growth-producing manner for all family members. We need to define the role of the man, the woman, and the child and help each member to understand clearly what their role is. For example, in the case of a single parent family, each member would need to know their role is to be carried out. We need to set up organizations and institutions to promote the training and development of our children to carry out these roles.

The problem in the family today is that it has lost sight of what the role of the man, the woman, and the child should be, regardless of the family model. If we could redefine these roles and then educate our children to carry out these roles, we could go a long way toward further development of a strong family. We cannot continue to use a model that stresses loose boundaries within the family, or allow our children to be totally educated in a system that mainly cares about the development and promotion of its own children. In this kind of system, our children will never receive maximum benefit. We need to control our schools and the agencies within our communities so that we can be thoroughly assured that certain values are being transmitted. At this point, our children are confused because they are given a set of values from white society, but then not allowed to participate fully.

Considering past family models. Educationally and historically, African Americans need to know where they came from and who they are. They need education that goes back further than when the Africans were brought to America on slave ships, which is a very small part of African history. Once we are able to understand where we came from, we can better understand where we are going. Education and training can further help in the development of the family in the twenty-first century.

African American Family Model in Slavery

When Africans were transplanted from Africa to the shores of the New World, the family was radically modified in terms of organization and structure. As a result of slavery and its consequences, the family deteriorated greatly. In slavery, men and women could not develop stable families because of the treatment of the white slave masters. Families could be pulled apart at any time to match the whimsies of their owners. The male was very unstable in his family role, out of necessity, because he had to be prepared to move at any time (Akbar, 1984).

The mother and child became the main family unit because men were traded and sold without their families. Men could not develop responsibility for their family (Frazier, 1939). In many cases even children were separated from their mothers. The fathers only had a biological function. The mother was responsible for the care of the children, and these children were considered hers. Many fathers failed to develop the feeling of responsibility for the children, since they did not have to care for and support the mother and children (Davie, 1949). A great number of slave fathers and freedman did act in the role of parent, nurturing their children to adulthood, when allowed the opportunity (Frazier, 1939). In slavery the man, woman and child were treated as property to be bought and sold by the slave owner. The man could not dictate what was to happen to his child, nor could the woman, though she had more negotiating power than he did.

African American Family Model in Present-Day America

Continuous patterns of unemployment and discrimination. The above historical antecedents are the forerunners of the so-called matricentric family organization found in African American communities throughout the United States. The situation in the family today has been passed on from generation to generation. Men still demonstrate an unstable pattern of family life, and simply have not become steady providers for their families in order to form more stable family units. Much of this is also related to continuous patterns of unemployment and discrimination. This leaves women to continue to take responsibility for rearing the children.

Concentration on negative models. Although African American males have many African American heroes at every level of American life, they usually do not consider these models as possibilities for themselves, instead concentrating on negative models (Jones, 1986). "They do this to such an extent that the male has become the most volatile—explosive element in the American society" (Riley, 1986, p. 24). He has an abundant supply of what Grier and Cobbs (1968) call rage. He is angry, frustrated, and violent; the biggest problem of all is that this rage is not harnessed to fight for necessary change in the system, but is turned against the community as well as himself (Riley, 1986). The statistics on homicides, suicides, use of drugs and the high school dropout rates bear out these facts. African Americans rate higher in these activities than any other group of people (1986).

A Twenty-First Century Model for the African American Family

The role of the African American male. He must be educated as to what roles must be played as husband and father. Some premarital preparation is necessary for the male. Also, preparation must be made for future marital roles by instilling pride in the heritage of the African American family as a patriarchal and patrilineal form of family organization. The male must learn to play a larger role in family activities, economic support, and socialization. The key is for the male to be able to provide successful husband/father role models for young males and transmit the role expectations that are necessary for meeting marital roles (Staples, 1970).

Men, in most cases, do not bother to spend the necessary time with their children in attempting to teach them the ways of the society as they know it. They expect their male children to learn from their mother, when it has been clearly demonstrated that, "Only a black man can teach a Black boy how to be a man, and black men seldom talk to their sons" (Hatchett, 1986, p. 36). The job of rearing the child, even when the man is present in the home, usually falls heavily upon the mother. The problem is that, "You can't overlook the fact that the mother can't be the total role model for a boy. She can't be the model for a transition into manhood" (Hare, 1986, p. 35). "Guidance from older men is very critical for the young male, and generally black adult males are the best enforcers of constructive channeling for the energy of young black boys" (Jones, 1986, p. 18). It is felt that without this guidance the young male will be dysfunctional. He usually will flourish if this guidance is provided.

The role of the African American female. The female needs to understand that historically there has been some deficits in the way the man has played his role in society, and that much of the way he performs has a historical significance and is a product of a conditioning process. Some of this process is related to slavery, subsequent discrimination, and lack of ability to get a job that would support a family. The female needs to learn that because of these factors the male requires a lot of support until he is able to fully regain the ability to carry out his role. She needs to understand that there is no inherent deficiency in him, and that with education and training he can begin to take responsibility for his role.

The female needs to understand that because of the male being perceived as threatening by the white society, he has been denied many opportunities (Jones, 1986). She has been perceived as less threatening and, therefore, has been given some of those same opportunities that have been denied the male. The female must learn not to abandon nor force him to leave home because of her discontent, but to be supportive and understanding of him, as well as keeping perspective on the historical conditioning process. She will play a tremendous role in determining whether or not the male and the family will survive into the twenty-first century and beyond.

Education and training of children and youth for family and community life. The responsibility for educating the children will be on the parents, and "Parents must make more of an effort to educate their children" (Hatchett, 1986, p. 46). Parents will have to provide a rite-of passage for their sons to grow into manhood. The father must teach his son how to be a man: Society in general cannot and will not perform this task (1986). The African American middle-class must lead the way toward helping young boys to become men, whereby other classes can follow in the tradition. The Black church, along with other institutions, needs to begin teaching young men and women how to conduct themselves. "Our homes must become learning institutions, places to energize and enlighten our children" (1986, p. 47). If not, we will face what the white media calls the disintegration or dissolution of the African American family structure. Education and training for family life and marital roles will be necessary for young children.

Clark (1983) believes that it is the overall quality of the family's lifestyle, and not composition, status, or other external family dynamics, that determines how well children will function. The family's contribution to a child's success comes from the parents' disposition and interpersonal relationships. Children get information on how to function from exposure to the home environment and the interaction that occurs there. One's survival and success knowledge is determined by one's own parents' ability, other family members, and parents' relationships within and outside the home. Communication behavior in the family works to produce children's motivations, expectations, and other competencies. The problem is that the necessary communication and interaction is likely not going to occur in many African American homes because there are too many obstacles against it. In other words, children must have appropriate role models from which to model their behavior. The problem is also that many African Americans, because of their hardships, are likely not adequate role models.

"The black family, institutions, and groups in the black community as social entities mutually affect one another's development and well-being" (Johnson, 1981). The relationship between family, institutions, organizations, programs, activities, and groups in the community can be enhanced by the working together of these units. This presupposes that there is an interrelationship between the community and the family; the family serves as a hub and is the center of the community. The African American has inherited a sense of community from its African ancestry. The community has comprised the basic spirit of African American people, and the individual functions for the good of the community.

It is the family that has the beginning, primary and lasting role in the socialization of the individual members of a group, community, society or nation. This means that through the family, the individual is prepared for life as a newcomer in the social, economic, physical, cultural and physical surroundings. Collective values, mores, patrimony, social and cultural habits, spiritual and technical knowledge, and survival skills, are all transmitted to the new person. The family is the first, and often the last social institution that an individual has contact with. It orients and influences the children who later become citizens, active in the affairs of the society (Johnson, 1981).

The family must then help to strengthen African American organizations and institutions by providing needed support to these institutions, agencies and groups. The family should be responsible for childrearing, giving specific attention to socialization and racial consciousness; economics; procreation; love and companionship; as well as basic physical needs (Johnson, 1981). Billingsley (1968) pointed out that: "These functions are highly interrelated with each other, and their effective execution depends not only on the structure of the family, but also on the structure of the society and the place of the family in that social structure" (p. 22).

It is felt by some authors that African Americans have transmitted negative self-images to their children, having been the victims of oppression. Others feel that this situation is changing, and African Americans are beginning to not transmit as much of these negatives as in the past (Johnson, 1981). It is understood that African Americans have had to socialize their children into a society that "Scorns them, rejects them, mistreats them, attempts to annihilate them, and labels them as inferior" (p. 38). The question then becomes: Can African families support, preserve, and perpetuate a society that does this to them?

The fact that African American individuals' self-esteem has been damaged by the factors of history deems it necessary for them to develop better ways of transmitting positive self-images to their children. If the family is to survive and grow strong, it will take the commitment of the family, community, organizations and institutions within the community to transmit the necessary positive self-image that will be required for the family to survive into the twenty-first century and beyond. African Americans must develop a sense of consciousness and survival for the community, rather than for the individual alone.

African Americans have developed a diffused mentality, being so diffused into white culture that they feel they can make it without having unity; a feeling that the individual takes precedent over everything else. We have to remember that African Americans have a history of lacking unity in the community that has kept them from everything but survival. Instead, we forget this simple fact and assume other attitudes, rather than having racial pride and consciousness. In some cases, African Americans reject themselves, their culture, and their heritage, refusing to identify with each other. This happens because of the many negatives that occur within the community (Johnson, 1981).

The family can control the images and stereotypes in the home as well as in the community; such as books, TV shows, pictures, and paintings. They can screen friends, language children use, as well as negative images (Johnson, 1981). Families can provide the economic resources necessary to strengthen the community. In order to survive as an economic entity, a community must have economic and social means available to it. In other words, members of the community must exchange labor, skills and talents for money and resources. They can, in turn, use money to purchase the goods and services they need as a family unit. African Americans have not engaged in this economic exchange successfully. They spent most of their money outside the community and pay for other groups to come into the community to provide goods and services.

Economically, African-Americans are a powerful group but cannot rally their resources to build their communities. "Too much of this money simply passes through black hands without resting in the black community or benefiting other blacks. In other communities, it is said that a dollar changes hands several times before leaving those communities" (Johnson, 1981, p. 43). African Americans do not support their financial institutions, and this must begin to happen if they are to advance as a group. African Americans will need to learn to spend their money on appropriate items, rather than clothes, shoes, and jewelry. If they spent their money more appropriately with African American individuals, they could control their own institutions and improve their family living conditions. African Americans, in some cases, equate material possessions with personal and psychological worth.

One of the failings of the community is that it has not taught its children the history of African American people. African American history was suppressed by whites for many generations, and African Americans themselves failed to adequately convey a sense of history to their children. It is said that a people lack direction without a sense of history. African Americans in many circles seem to believe that there is something shameful about their history that makes it not worthy of being passed on. Knowledge of our history will give us total understanding of how we have developed as a people, what we face in terms of opposition, what we must do to continue to survive as a people and keep our families strong. We have always been able to thrive in a hostile environment, but the question is: how much longer? We do know that, when given the opportunity, we have always made a good showing, even in the face of overwhelming odds.

Summary

The issue is not what family model will provide the best setting for the development of our children, and thus the continuation of the race, as well as provide nurturing for the adults in the situation while meeting their needs. The issue is what kind of training we can provide for our children, regardless of the family model, that will ensure the survival of the race and the development of family life. It should be maintained that if the proper training is given to children, it will not matter what the family type or model. The main issue confronting the family today are education and training for family, economic, social, and political life; relevant to the history of African American people, as well as their present-day survival needs. These, more than any other factors, will assure a strong family for the twenty-first century and beyond.

References

Akbar, N. (1984). Chains and images of psychological slavery. New Jersey: New Mind Productions.

Billingsley, A. (1968). Black families in white America. New Jersey: Prentice-Hall, Inc.

Clark, R. (1983). Family life and school achievement. Chicago: The University of Chicago Press.

Davie, M.R. (1949). Negroes in American society. New York: McGraw-Hill.

Frazier, F.E. (1939). The Negro family in the United States. Chicago: University of Chicago Press.

Grier, W.H., & Cobbs, P.M. (1968). Black rage. New York: Basic Books, Inc.

Hare, N. (1986). Interview. Crisis, 93, 35.

Hatchett, D. (1986). … A conflict of reasons and remedies. Crisis, 93, 36.

Johnson, R.C. (1981). The Black family and Black community development. The Journal of Black Psychology, 8, 35-52.

Jones, K. (1986). The Black male in Jeopardy. Crisis, 93, 18.

Riley, N. (1986). Footnotes of a culture at risk. Crisis, 93, 23-28.

Staples, R.E. (1970). Educating the Black male at various class levels for marital roles. The family coordinator, 19, 164-165.

Chapter 14

Conclusion

There is always debate from a large percentage of the population when considering that the history of the African American family has consequences for its present behavior. It is difficult for those who would argue this point to believe that slavery had the devastating effect that is claimed in this book; it is even harder for them to understand how some pre-colonial African values have been passed on as well. Most African Americans find it difficult to consider these facts, especially when most of them want to forget about slavery and simply write it off as a bad experience by our forefathers. We do not like to be reminded of slavery. People cannot understand or believe that what happened so many years ago could become embedded in the cultural processes—with no relation to genetics—and be maintained over generations.

We forget that once a people have been conditioned, they tend to pass their values and culture to their offspring, regardless of whether these characteristics are good or bad. Through generations of slavery, the African American acquired dysfunctional behavior that has been handed down through the generations. It is maintained that this is the reason that we have witnessed the strain in the African American family. A dysfunctional process set in motion can only imitate itself, which means that the problem will increase with each generation. This has happened with the African American family until the situation has reached epidemic proportions.

If there is a desire to return the family back to a "normal" state, it is necessary, over successive generations, to develop a strategy to intervene in this deterioration process. It will be difficult because the African American tends to resist the methods of suggested intervention; mainly in education, counseling and psychotherapy. A strategy such as the one in this book must then be developed to overcome this resistance.

We must also look toward the future and consider what must be done to return to traditional values which have kept us strong, yet pliable. In addition, there is a need to develop new strategies and to be involved in research that might help us to further draw conclusions about how we can maintain a strong functional family for the future. It is important to develop our families, communities, and institutions because one cannot be strong without the others.

This will not be easy, and we will all have to make an effort to concern ourselves with our own family, as well as the families of other African Americans in the immediate and the larger community. The time is now—we can no longer postpone the task of working to improve the situation of our families. If we continue to maintain a policy of diffusion, claiming that *its every man for himself*, the future will be disastrous. We might then come face to face with what the media labels as "the vanishing African American family," and as it describes the African American male, "the endangered species," or "the African American male in crisis." The survival of the entire African American species may be endangered, if a concentrated effort is not made toward improving the situation of the family.

After reading this book, it is hoped that those African Americans who feel that there is something wrong in their lives but just cannot get in touch with the problem, will seek help from someone who can provide the necessary psychotherapy. This will be a big step since it is difficult for most African Americans to arrive at this kind of conclusion. In addition, a large number of us have gone through the kind of changes and trauma, which will necessitate help from someone if we are to put our lives together.

NOTES

NOTES

NOTES

NOTES

Made in the USA
Monee, IL
04 November 2026

67375679R00164